T ■ H ■ E
SPIRITUAL
GIFTS
HANDBOOK

T·H·E

SPIRITUAL

GIFTS

HANDBOOK

*The Complete Guide
to Discovering & Using
Your Spiritual Gifts*

BRUCE W. BLACK

LOIZEAUX
Neptune, New Jersey

Unless otherwise stated, Scripture quotations in this book are taken from
The New King James Version.
Copyright © 1979, 1980, 1982, Thomas Nelson, Inc.

Verses marked (NIV) are taken from the
HOLY BIBLE, NEW INTERNATIONAL VERSION ®.
Copyright © 1973, 1978, 1984 by International Bible Society.
Used by permission of Zondervan Publishing House. All rights reserved.
The "NIV" and "New International Version" trademarks are registered in the
United States Patent and Trademark Office by International Bible Society.
Use of either trademark requires the permission of International Bible Society.

Verse marked (TLB) is taken from *The Living Bible* © 1971.
Used by permission of Tyndale House Publishers, Inc.,
Wheaton, IL 60189. All rights reserved.

Verses marked (KJV) are taken from the King James version.

Appendix C includes material published by
Christian Development Resources,
2850 Kalamazoo Avenue SE, Grand Rapids, MI 49560.
Used by permission.

Library of Congress Cataloging-in-Publication Data

Black, Bruce W., 1943–
The spiritual gifts handbook / by Bruce W. Black.
Includes bibliographical references.
ISBN 0-87213-058-4 (pbk.)
1. Gifts, Spiritual.   I. Title.
BT767.3.B54   1995
234'.13—dc20   94-43446

Printed in the United States of America
10 9 8 7 6 5 4 3 2 1

DEDICATION

✥

This work is dedicated

to my loving wife and understanding family,
whose sacrifices and encouragement
enabled me to develop this handbook,

and to Naomi and Bob Bergen,
whose expression of their gifts of serving,
including hospitality,
made the completion of the project possible.

CONTENTS

FOREWORD

S ince the 1960s numerous books and articles have been written concerning spiritual gifts. Although many authors have addressed the conceptual aspects of the subject, few have dealt with the practical aspects. In *The Spiritual Gifts Handbook* Dr. Black has produced an excellent blend of concept and application.

In the conceptual realm he has demonstrated why spiritual gifts are so critical to the life, function, and growth of the church; he has explained what spiritual gifts are, formed definitions of the various gifts, and addressed the issue of the cessation of some gifts. In the practical realm he has developed methods believers can use to discern how they have been gifted and to evaluate the accuracy of their discernment; he has also compiled specific suggestions of ways believers can use their gifts in ministry.

Because the subject of spiritual gifts is controversial, not everyone will agree with all of Dr. Black's conclusions. Hopefully those who disagree with his definitions or his list of gifts present today will not reject the entire book, for it has the potential to make a significant contribution to the health of every Bible-believing church.

RENALD E. SHOWERS

PREFACE

W hy would anyone want to write another book on spiritual gifts? The number of books on the subject easily tops two hundred. Certainly it has all been said before...or has it?

The volume of material already written about spiritual gifts is second only to that written about the family. But, with few exceptions, this mountain of material deals with one aspect: glossolalia, pro and con. There are piles of information available on tongues and the cessation of gifts, but a surprisingly small amount on mercy, giving, administration, serving, and helps.

There is a shortage of the kind of material that takes us beyond the lists of gifts (short, long, extended, micro-, macro-) and shows us how the gifts should work in our lives. The church needs a "how to" manual to help the individual believer discover his/her gift(s) and then use it (them) for the profit of the body of Christ and the glory of God. This handbook was written to fill that need. Going beyond the lists, *The Spiritual Gifts Handbook* provides user-friendly definitions of the gifts. Then going beyond the definitions, it provides a step-by-step approach to aid the reader in discovering his gifts and using them.

Theologians argue over the exact number of gifts that are extant today, and each of us is the product of a theological bias. But we would agree that there *are* spiritual gifts resident in the lives of all believers. Yet the church of Jesus Christ is bereft of the full *use* of these gifts. God wants to use these gifts to profit the whole body.

As a believer *you* are gifted. So discover your gifts! Use your gifts so that the body of Christ will grow! That is my heartcry. You need to be serving in your church. You have tools (your spiritual gifts) that God wants to use. My prayer is that this handbook will enable you to use your gifts.

INTRODUCTION

I f we could only keep one-quarter of the people who visit our church, we would be bursting at the seams." I am quoting myself, my elders, and countless other pastors and church leaders. This statement, which underscores one of the abiding frustrations of pastoring a church, needs careful scrutiny. If the statement is true of your church and mine, one of the keys to church growth is already within our grasp: keep those who visit our services. If we could somehow stop the "turnstile effect," we could enhance the kingdom of God, produce more hands and feet to do His work, and increase the labor force of harvesters.

My immediate concern is not for those who attend one service and decide not to return. My concern is for those newcomers who are contacted by our visitation outreach, stay for a while...and *then* move on—often for no identifiable reason.

What might the reason be? Part of the answer is implied in Ephesians 4:16, which spells out Paul's concept of church life:

> Under his [Christ's] direction the whole body is fitted together perfectly, and *each part in its own special way helps the other parts,* so that the whole body is healthy and growing and full of love (TLB, italics added).

In Paul's view of the church, all members are involved in service and ministry. I really believe the lack of such involvement is the reason for the "turnstile effect." Generally if people do not become involved in service of some sort (ushering, singing in the choir, or participating in some other small group), they leave—often without realizing why. Fewer newcomers would leave if they were encouraged to discover, cultivate, and use their divinely-endowed spiritual gifts, and through their use, become plugged into ministry.

I have not reached any startling conclusions regarding the "turnstile effect." My belief is based on Biblical principles laid down by Paul for the New Testament church. To encourage a return to these principles, I have written this *Spiritual Gifts Handbook*. My desire is that after my readers have digested and followed the principles in this book, they will have a ready, excited, and positive response to the question: How are you plugged into ministry for Christ in your local church?

1
GOD'S BLUEPRINT

From him [Christ] the whole body, joined and held together
by every supporting ligament, grows and builds itself up in
love, as each part does its work (Ephesians 4:16, NIV).

Have you ever wondered why the church of Jesus Christ seems
to be suffering from "iron-deficiency anemia," and is in desperate need of a double dose of spiritual Geritol? Although there
are notable exceptions, in general the evangelical church in
America is lethargic, anemic, and ineffective. This malady is
due to several factors, not the least of which is a lack of opposition.

We live in a climate of religious freedom where the church is
not persecuted and is almost respected. This freedom furnishes
us with an unparalleled opportunity to spread the gospel of Christ
without governmental interference. The benefits of living in a
free society are many, but there are drawbacks. The lack of opposition tends to cause us to lose our cutting edge. The advent
of peace and prosperity can lead to apathy.

Israel was reminded in Deuteronomy 6 that hard times, persecution by enemies, and catastrophes would not turn them away
from God. After Moses talked about the blessings and peace
that would be theirs once they had taken Canaan, he said, "*Then*
beware, lest you forget the Lord" (Deuteronomy 6:12).

The climate of our society undoubtedly contributes to the lethargy we see today in our churches. Another factor contributing
to this anemia forms the backbone of this volume: *the church of
Jesus Christ is stumbling forward instead of sprinting because
it is not proceeding according to God's prescribed plan.* What
is God's plan? What is His blueprint for church growth?

Every church has a philosophy of ministry. Sometimes this

philosophy is carefully explained in the church bylaws or con-
stitution. Sometimes no formula is written in black and white,
but the philosophy exists all the same and is followed meticu-
lously.

A church's philosophy of ministry is the plan that it espouses
and follows to achieve its goals. The plan answers the question,
What can we do to make our church grow? The response to this
question determines the route to be followed and most of the
stops along the way. Once the course is laid, the church is on
"automatic pilot." Once a philosophy is adopted, it remains in
place, untouched, for decades. The church will make a few de-
tours, but overall it will doggedly follow its course like a receiver following a homing device. To challenge one's church's
philosophy is often perceived as tantamount to challenging a
tenet of Scripture.

Since its philosophy will dictate the path a church will follow, it is crucial that the formula be correct. But sometimes a
church is like the newly married woman who was preparing a
ham dinner for her in-laws. As her husband watched, she deftly
hacked off the end of the ham before she put it in the pan to be
cooked. When he asked why she hacked off the end, she re-
plied, "My mother always did it that way." When the bride was
pressed by her husband for a more definitive answer, she called
her mother and asked her. The mother responded, "Why, dear,
that's the way we have always prepared ham. My mother always did it that way." Now the bride was really curious, so she
called her grandmother and asked her. "Grandma, why did you
always cut off the end of the ham before cooking it?" The grandmother responded, "I always did it that way because my pan
was too small for the ham." We need to be sure that our philosophy of ministry is based on something more concrete than
the size of our grandmother's baking pan!

The good news is that we don't have to rely on our own philosophy of ministry and hope that it is the correct one. God has
given us His formula. All we need to do is incorporate it into
our own church formula and then implement it. We find God's
formula in Ephesians 4:16 where Paul stated that the church
"builds itself up in love, as each part does its work" (NIV).

In Ephesians 4 Paul compared the church of Jesus Christ to a physical body with Him being the head and the members being the other individual parts. Paul used the same imagery in Colossians, Philippians, and his other Epistles. The analogy is excellent because of the many similarities between a physical body and the church. In 1 Corinthians 12 Paul made the point that the parts of the body have varied functions and each part is vital to the health of the body.

Obviously there are some parts without which the physical body can exist. The longevity of man is due in large measure to the number of "removable parts" that God has placed in the body. The body can make do without one lung, one kidney, one eye, or even both legs. But if one of these "removable parts" is missing, the body cannot function as efficiently as it was intended to function. For the physical body to be healthy and continue to function smoothly, all its parts must carry out their individual tasks. Similarly the body of Christ has no extraneous parts. Every part is needed and equipped to fulfill a particular role. Every part must fulfill its God-ordained role if the body is to maintain good health and function as the church was intended to function.

When we look at the context of Paul's analogy, we see the relationship between the functioning of the body and spiritual gifts. In 1 Corinthians 12:12-27 Paul talked about the body of Christ in general. In these verses he used the word *one* twelve times and the word *body* eighteen times, emphasizing that there is only *one body* of Christ. All believers are part of the one body. Paul stated in a variety of ways that the body of Christ is the sum of all its parts, and that every single part is necessary to the smooth operation of that body. Directly following this discourse on the unity of the body and the importance of each member of the body of Christ, Paul listed several spiritual gifts.

In Romans 12 Paul followed the same train of thought. First he stated that the church is the body of Christ and believers are the members that make up this body (12:4-5). Then he immediately added, "Having then [spiritual] gifts..." (12:6), and proceeded to elaborate on several of these gifts. In both 1 Corinthians 12 and Romans 12, when Paul talked about the body of Christ, the subject of spiritual gifts was not far behind.

In Ephesians 4 Paul turned from the theme of the body of Christ being the sum of all its parts. In this chapter his emphasis was on the purpose and smooth operation of the body of Christ. In 4:11-16 he sketched out the intended normal functioning of this body. Paul started by listing the God-ordained leadership He has set in place for the establishment and continued operation of His church (4:11). The list includes five titles: apostle, prophet, evangelist, pastor, and teacher. In the original syntax, the last two titles are combined (pastor/teacher), thus making the number of offices four.

A further examination of these titles and the functions of the offices leads us to a couple of conclusions. The purpose of the first two offices (apostle and prophet) was to lay the foundation of the church. The apostles and prophets were the Titan rocket boosters that blasted the church off the launching pad and into orbit. Once insertion was achieved, the rocket boosters were jettisoned, and thruster rockets propelled the vehicle on its journey. The evangelists and pastor/teachers are the thruster rockets. These last two offices are intended to continue the operation of the founded organism.

Paul followed up this list of titles with a job description for these offices (Ephesians 4:12). The King James version gives the impression that the task of this God-ordained leadership is threefold: for perfecting, for ministry, for edifying. This translation suggests that the task of church leadership is (1) to cause the saints to mature, (2) to minister to those in the body, and (3) to edify or build up the church. But when we examine the verse in the original language, we arrive at a far different understanding. Capturing the true meaning, the New International Version states that the task of church leadership is "to prepare God's people for works of service, so that the body of Christ may be built up."

The New King James Version (Ephesians 4:12) speaks of "equipping" the saints. The word translated "equipping" *(katartizmos)* is colorful. It means "to restore, to make anew, to mend." Depending on the context, the word could mean "to make ready again for use; to fold and mend nets, readying them for the next thrust into the deep; [or] to rig or fully prepare a ship for a journey."[1] In the context of the church the word indicates that the task of leadership is to take useless broken lives that have been repaired through conversion and prepare them for service by completely outfitting them with a knowledge of what their spiritual gifts are and how to use the gifts.

Paul had a very special type of service in mind for believers: "the work of ministry." The word translated "service/ministry" has the connotation of "very personal service rendered to another…a service of love."[2]

The task of church leadership then is to equip the members of the body of Christ with a knowledge of their gifts so that believers can minister to one another in love. If the members use their gifts, the inevitable result will be that the body of Christ will build *itself* up in love. Contrary to popular belief, the pastor's task is not to make the church grow. His job is to equip the saints and *they* cause the church to grow. What really produces qualitative and quantitative growth is the ministry of the saints to those within the body and those outside as well. Certainly the church leader is a factor—on either the plus or the minus side—but the real Scriptural key to growth is the mobilization of the congregation into a body that ministers.

This concept is clearly stated in Ephesians 4:16. There Paul showed us the way God intends the body of Christ to function. That verse provides God's blueprint for church maintenance and growth. God intends His church to be a ministering body where each part does its share and makes its contribution so that the entire body functions smoothly.

This Biblical concept seems foreign to the twentieth-century church of Jesus Christ. The church we see today is different from Paul's picture of a healthy church. The average church today is not the ministering body Paul described. The average church depends on staff, program, and facilities to produce growth. The result is an unhealthy body that functions abnormally, and limps at best. The church has become a body whose legs are only able to shuffle. The arms work, sort of, but not together. There are circulatory problems because only some of the arteries feel like pushing along the blood. Strange sounds are coming from the left ear because it really wants to be the mouth. The hands hold a whole box of new parts that don't know where they fit or how to be of use.

The "patient" is sick! In fact she is on "life support." All of her functions are being performed by outside forces. Running around in white coats are a group of medical specialists called "staff." They are desperately trying to do everything the body is not doing, instead of getting that box of new parts functioning so the body can get well. How do I know? I have a whole closet full of white coats. The real clincher is that the patient seems all too willing to let the staff do the body's work instead of insisting that the specialists make the body well.

There are probably several reasons for this present-day phenomenon. Part of the problem is that we live in a world with a TV mentality. We sit in front of televisions or computers or video games and watch them "do their thing." We expect the same when we go to church. We arrive on Sunday morning and say, silently if not audibly, "OK, I'm here; entertain me." Instead of coming to serve and minister, we come to sit and watch and allow worship to "happen" to us. Instead of coming expecting to be prepared and equipped to accomplish works of service, we come expecting to be entertained, or preached to, or made to feel good. No doubt this mindset is partially to blame for the moving away of the church from God's mandated blueprint.

Another part of the problem—and this consideration may be even more endemic to the sickness—is that parishioners may not know *how* to put Ephesians 4:16 into operation in their lives. They may read the verse in a variety of translations and hear it enthusiastically expounded from the pulpit, but then nothing happens. They know that the body is the sum of all its parts; they know that each part must do its share; they know that God intends every believer to have a ministry. But they are left high and dry with no practical suggestions or illustrations of what Paul had in mind.

Many believers do not minister because they view the list of spiritual gifts as very narrow and only applying to the elite. When the phrase *spiritual gifts* is mentioned, people tend to think of pastor and teacher, but are hard pressed to add to this list.

Believers who don't fit into one of these two slots conclude that they are not gifted and have no place to serve. But the complete list includes very few gifts that are relegated to leadership positions.

The manifestation of a gift can be as simple as a telephone call to encourage someone who is hurting or an afternoon spent helping a senior citizen with yard work. A gift is being used when the right person takes over the chairmanship of a committee or organizes a particular project. The list of ways spiritual gifts can be used is limited only by our imaginations and the specific needs within our particular assembly of believers. For practical suggestions for identifying and using spiritual gifts, read the following chapters of this handbook.

A very successful midwestern college basketball coach was asked by a Chicago reporter, "What has the emphasis and popular appeal of college and professional football done for the physical fitness of America?" His answer was immediate. "Absolutely nothing! Football is twenty-two men on the field that desperately need rest and ninety thousand in the stands that desperately need exercise!" This sport is a graphic illustration of the church today. In most churches 90 percent of the work is done by 10 percent of the people. To change these percentages, each member of the body of Christ will have to involve himself in ministry by using the special tools God has given him: his spiritual gifts. The exercise of spiritual gifts has from the beginning been *God's* plan, *His* blueprint for growth.

2

SPIRITUAL GIFTS

The term *spiritual gifts* has stirred up controversy in the Christian community for many years. At the time I was doing research for this handbook there were over two hundred books on the subject of gifts. In all this accumulation of material there was very little information about the gifts themselves. Most of the books either promoted the charismatic movement or preached against it. This handbook avoids the gridlock of charge and countercharge.

What are spiritual gifts? The Greek term uniformly translated "spiritual gifts" is *charismata*, from which we get the English terms "charisma" and "charismatic." The Greek language has at least three words meaning "gift/giving," and each has a different connotation. Two of these terms, *doma* and *dosis*, emphasize the *act* of giving. *Charismata* emphasizes the *nature* of the gift.[1] Derived from the common Greek word *charis* ("grace"), *charismata* literally means "grace-gifts." Such gifts are by nature totally undeserved, provided by grace.

The use of the term *charismata* is not restricted in the New Testament to passages on spiritual gifts. The term is used in Romans 6:23 to describe eternal life as the gracious gift of God. Paul used the term again in 2 Corinthians 1:11 to describe God's providential care for him. In both cases the emphasis is the same: the gracious nature of the particular gift in view. In most instances, however, *charismata* refers to spiritual gifts, and the term is usually followed by a list of particular gifts.

Most authors describe spiritual gifts in similar terms. John Walvoord wrote, "Spiritual gifts are divinely given capacities to perform useful functions for God, especially in the area of service."[2] Peter Wagner wrote, "Spiritual gifts are special attributes given by the Holy Spirit to every member of the Body of Christ according to God's grace for use within the context of the Body."[3] All of the definitions speak of the source of the gifts, the recipients of the gifts, and the purpose of the gifts.

THE SOURCE

The term *spiritual gifts* itself tells us the source: the Spirit. A closer look at 1 Corinthians 12 will convince us of this truth.

Introducing the subject in 12:1, the King James text says, "Now concerning spiritual *gifts*..." "Gifts" is in italics because the word was not in the original text, but was added by the translators to complete the sense of the statement. In this instance they did us a disservice. Here the word translated "spiritual gifts" is not *charismata,* the usual term thus translated. The original word is *pneumatikia,* which means "things pertaining to the (Holy) Spirit." Paul was really saying, "Now concerning those things pertaining to the Spirit..." Spiritual gifts or grace-gifts fall under the general heading of the work of the Holy Spirit in the life of the believer.

The Corinthians misunderstood the work of the Holy Spirit in the life of the believer. This misunderstanding manifested itself in aberrations in the area of spiritual gifts. First Corinthians was written by Paul to curb these and other excesses. We need to remember that the Epistle is corrective in nature. It is not a thoroughly comprehensive statement on spiritual gifts, but a letter telling the Corinthians what they were doing wrong.

Having introduced the subject, Paul went on in 1 Corinthians 12:8-11 to deal with the source of spiritual gifts. In 12:8-9 (KJV) Paul said four separate times that these gifts are "by" the Spirit. The King James version gives the impression that Paul used the same wording each time, but he actually used three different constructions to tell us the same story.

The first "by" in 12:8 (KJV) is a translation of the preposition *dia,* one of the simplest expressions of agency. *Dia* means "by" in the sense of "through, by means of."[4] This construction tells us that God the Father is the ultimate source of these gifts and God the Holy Spirit is the means through which they are given to man.

The second "by" in 12:8 (KJV) is the preposition *kata*, which means "according to."[5] This construction tells us that the Holy Spirit is the One who distributes these gifts.

The third construction, used twice in 12:9, is the common preposition *en*, which is another common expression of instrumentality. Paul used *en* to indicate that the Holy Spirit is the instrument through which the believer receives these gifts.

Did Paul use three separate constructions for the sake of variety, or for emphasis? Because 1 Corinthians 12 is corrective, dealing with excesses in the church, I would lean toward the second explanation. Paul emphatically underlined the relationship between the Holy Spirit and His gifts so that no one could misinterpret his words.

In 12:11 Paul showed that the gifts and the Holy Spirit are inseparable. Referring to the spiritual gifts listed in 12:8-10, he wrote, "One and the same Spirit works all these [spiritual gifts], distributing to each one individually as He wills."

The verb translated "works" in 12:11 is *energeo*, from which we get "energy, energize." Paul's emphasis here is clear. There is only one Holy Spirit and it is this one Holy Spirit who distributes these gifts. The Holy Spirit is the energizer of these gifts.

The verb translated "distributing" in 12:11 is *diaroun*, which means "to distribute or divide among."[6] Notice that the subject of this verb is the Holy Spirit. Grace-gifts are dispensed by the Holy Spirit of God. He does the distributing.

We are also told in 1 Corinthians 12:11 that gifts are distributed "as He wills." A couple of Greek words can be translated "wills." In this verse Paul used *boulomai*. The noun form, *boule*, refers to the determinate inviolable counsel of God, settled before the foundation of the world. *Boule* is linked to God's sovereignty and has the force of a divine decree.[7] We can infer that God determined the "who" and "what" of spiritual gifts before the world began. God determined what our spiritual gifts would be even before we were! God the Holy Spirit is the sovereign source of spiritual gifts. We have what we have by divine decree. God, not you and I, determines what we have for our spiritual gift mix. We cannot change His decree. If God has given me the gift of administration, my prayer for the gift of evangelism will not avail. God's sovereignty and omniscience are the basis of our gifts. These endowments can be received only as gifts of God's grace.

THE RECIPIENTS

Only believers in Jesus Christ are the recipients of these divine bestowals. Every believer is equipped for service at the time of his salvation; he is endowed sovereignly by the Holy Spirit with spiritual gifts. Since the Holy Spirit is the sole source and sovereign dispenser of spiritual gifts, we can conclude that only those who know Him can receive these gifts from Him.

In 1 Corinthians 2:11 Paul clearly stated that the things of God can only be understood by one possessing the Spirit of God. In 2:14 he added that the natural man—the man outside of Christ, the man ruled by his senses, the unregenerate man—cannot receive the things of the Spirit of God because they are "spiritually discerned." *Pneumatikia* ("things pertaining to the Spirit" in 1 Corinthians 12:1) would be beyond the grasp and comprehension of the natural man.

In Romans 12 Paul made the assumption that only believers—and all believers—are recipients of spiritual gifts. His use of "we" and "every one" in 12:4-5 (KJV) indicates that he was talking only about believers, and about all believers; and the phrase "having then gifts" in 12:6 must refer to the pronoun "we" in the previous verse. Paul accepted as a matter of fact that every believer in Rome was already a possessor of spiritual gifts. The only qualification for having these gifts was membership in the body of Christ.

First Corinthians 12 leads us to the same conclusions about the recipients of spiritual gifts. Paul began the chapter with an emphasis on the unity of the body of Christ, and in 12:13 he wrote, "By one Spirit we were all baptized into one body." Every believer in Jesus Christ, at the moment of his salvation, is placed into (the literal meaning of "baptized") the body of Christ. This baptism occurs only once in the life of the believer and is not repeated. In 12:13 this baptism is spoken of as a *fait accompli,* a finished act in the life of the believer. We are never commanded to be baptized by the Spirit. This baptism is God's automatic response to our saving faith in His Son.

Every believer (notice the word "all" in 12:13) is baptized by the Holy Spirit, placed into the body of Christ. If we read between the lines, we understand that there were those in Corinth who used certain gifts as the criteria for being in the body of Christ. Paul negated this false concept in a hurry!

When the Holy Spirit places us into the body of Christ, he endows us with spiritual gifts so that we are equipped to function properly. Not all have the same gift, but each has at least one. At the end of 1 Corinthians 12 Paul listed several gifts that believers possess. The proximity of this list to the statement regarding Spirit baptism suggests that the baptism and the bestowal of gifts are concurrent.

THE PURPOSE

The purpose of spiritual gifts was spelled out by Paul in 1 Corinthians 12:7, and in one word that purpose is "profit." The text makes it clear that the profit is to be mutual. John Stott said that the purpose of these gifts is "not to help, comfort, and strengthen self [the recipient] but others."[8] L. I. Sweet, among others, agreed. He wrote, "Charismata are gifts to individuals, but they are never meant for private use....They are not for personal enjoyment, employment, or edification, but for service to others."[9]

To miss this allocentric (others-centered) emphasis is to miss an important key to the understanding and use of spiritual gifts. Any gift that is not exercised for the purpose of profiting others is not being used properly. Take a look at the Corinthian church to see what happens when the activity of church members is not allocentric in scope. In Corinth gifts became badges of spirituality and the result was absolute havoc. The purpose of our gifts is to benefit the body of Christ. They are to be used to minister to others, to help others, to edify others, to teach others, to shepherd others, to exhort others, and to provide for the needs of others in the body of Christ. As Earl McQuay pointed out, spiritual gifts are "tools not toys."[10]

If we liken members of the church to a baseball team, we can compare spiritual gifts to the equipment provided by management for the purpose of playing the game. We cannot continue the analogy much further, however, because in the Christian life no one is on the bench; everyone has to participate. The New Testament church is all playing field; there is no place for spectators. The Holy Spirit needs all the gifts He bestows to be operative so that the body of Christ can function normally.

Peter agreed with Paul that the scope of the use of gifts is allocentric. First Peter 4:10 says, "As each one has received a gift, minister it to one another." The word translated "gift" is *charisma* (from the same root as *charismata*), which refers to a grace-gift or spiritual gift, and the term translated "minister" refers to personal service rendered to another in agape-love.

Peter added a new thought: an accountability factor. He said that we are to minister to one another through our gifts "as good stewards of the manifold grace of God." The picture of the steward in Scripture is always the same. He is entrusted with assets to be invested in the owner's absence. Upon the owner's return, the steward gives an accounting and he is evaluated on the basis of his faithfulness in handling the assets. Likewise God has entrusted us with assets—spiritual gifts—that He wants us to put to use in the body of Christ. He is looking for a return on His investment, and when He comes He will ask for an accounting.

3
SCRIPTURAL LISTS

When we search the Scriptures for material on spiritual gifts, we find it in four major passages. We find two lists of gifts in 1 Corinthians 12, one list in Romans 12, and a list of gifted offices in Ephesians 4. In addition we find an overview in 1 Peter 4. Let's look at the four passages where specific gifts are mentioned and compare the lists.

Ephesians 4:11	1 Corinthians 12:28	1 Corinthians 12:8-10	Romans 12:6-8
Apostle	Apostle		
Prophet	Prophet	Prophecy	Prophecy
Evangelist			
Pastor			
Teacher	Teacher		Teaching
			Exhortation
		Word of Wisdom	
		Word of Knowledge	
		Faith	
	Miracles	Miracles	
	Healings	Healings	
	Helps		Ministering
			Giving
	Administration		Leading
			Mercy
		Discerning of Spirits	
	Tongues	Tongues	
		Interpretation of Tongues	

Notice the disparity between Paul's lists in 1 Corinthians and his lists in Ephesians and Romans. In Ephesians 4 Paul listed the gifted offices that God ordained for the foundation and continued edification of His church. Other gifts are not listed because of the context. Paul's purpose in Ephesians 4 was to give an overview of the task of leadership, not to describe gifts bestowed on individual members.

The two lists in 1 Corinthians 12 (one near the beginning of the chapter and one toward the end) are longer than the lists in Ephesians and Romans. Only the lists in 1 Corinthians include the "miraculous" gifts (miracles, tongues, healings, word of knowledge, word of wisdom, discerning of spirits). Why? Part of the answer lies in the tone and purpose of 1 Corinthians. The church at Corinth was rife with problems, not the least of which was their misunderstanding and misuse of spiritual gifts. Paul's letter was intended to correct their aberrations. He was dealing with areas where the Corinthian Christians had gone off on tangents and had entertained false concepts and ideas.

The list in Romans 12 is of the "speaking and serving" variety. Paul's letter to the Roman believers is different from his other Epistles. He did not found the church at Rome; he had never been there; he had not met many in the congregation. Neither did he have a full picture of their doctrinal base, so in his letter he explained the great doctrines of the Christian faith. Therefore Romans 1:1–15:13 is a doctrinal treatise and his text on spiritual gifts is a straightforward statement on the subject. If the miraculous gifts left out of the Roman list were important for the church of Christ, Paul certainly would have included them in this doctrinal treatise.

The overview in 1 Peter 4 simply mentions the classifications of speaking and serving gifts. Why did Peter have so little to say on the subject? Perhaps his readers were already familiar with the truths about spiritual gifts. Perhaps the subject was easily understood and needed no further explanation. Or perhaps among Peter's readers there were no excesses, and no corrective instruction was warranted.

If we combine the four lists on page 29 and delete the duplications, we form a master list:

Apostle
Prophet
Evangelist
Pastor
Teacher
Exhortation
Word of Wisdom
Word of Knowledge
Faith
Miracles
Healings
Helps (Ministering)
Giving
Administration (Leadership)
Mercy
Discerning of Spirits
Tongues
Interpretation of Tongues

These gifts are usually arranged in three categories. Unfortunately most of the suggested formats only take into account the list in 1 Corinthians 12:8-10. Lester Sumrall classified the gifts as follows: revelatory gifts (word of wisdom, word of knowledge, discerning of spirits); power gifts (faith, healings, miracles); and inspiration gifts (prophecy, tongues, and interpretation of tongues).[1] Ralph Riggs used almost the same breakdown: revelatory gifts, power gifts, and gifts of utterance.[2] Donald Gee suggested only two categories: gifts of utterance and gifts of power.[3] I propose the following threefold classification:

Sign/Revelatory Gifts	Speaking Gifts	Serving Gifts
Apostle	Prophet - secondary	Faith
Prophet - primary	Evangelist	Helps / Ministering
Word of Wisdom	Pastor	Giving
Word of Knowledge	Teacher	Administration/Leadership
Tongues	Exhortation	Mercy
Interpretation of Tongues		
Discerning of Spirits		
Healings		
Miracles		

Some people think the individual spiritual gifts listed in Scripture do not comprise a complete inventory. Peter Wagner, for example, said, "No list is complete. Apparently, they were not intended to be complete, but only suggest categories of gifts God gives."[4] If Wagner's view of an open-ended list is correct, everything anyone does in the area of Christian service could be classified as the exercise of a spiritual gift. But if everything done in the name of the Lord is the exercise of a spiritual gift, the designation is meaningless. We must limit our view to those divine enablements named in Scripture. John Owen defined spiritual gifts as "that without which the church cannot subsist in the world, nor can believers be useful to one another and the rest of mankind."[5] These necessary gifts, labeled *charismata,* form the Scriptural list.[6]

The question remains, Are all nineteen of these gifts for today? My contention is that sign gifts are not. They ceased when the offices they were given to validate ceased. The foundation of the apostles and prophets was laid by the end of the first century, and the sign gifts that validated them were not needed after the foundation was laid. The revelatory gifts have also ceased. They served as the means of delivering the New Testament, but once the Canon was completed, the purpose of revelatory gifts was fulfilled. For more information on sign/revelatory gifts, see appendix A.

The speaking and serving gifts *are* for today. They are described in detail in the next two chapters. As you read the descriptions, you may realize which gifts have been given to you.

4

SPEAKING GIFTS

Speaking gifts include prophecy, evangelism, shepherding, teaching, and exhortation. As you read the definitions of each one, ask yourself, "Is this perhaps a gift I possess?"

PROPHECY

Most noncharismatics agree that the office of prophet—in its primary sense—has ceased. This foundational office (Ephesians 2:20; Hebrews 2:3-4) ceased with the passing of those who were contemporaries of Christ. (See appendix A.) However, the question remains, Is there a sense in which the gift of prophecy is preserved today? Many see the office of prophet as extant in a secondary sense. My opinion is that today the work of the prophet is carried on by the pastor/teacher. But because of my adamant claim to fallibility and my utmost respect for those who disagree, I will present the view of continuance here.

Let me emphasize that *if* the gift is extant, it has continued only in a secondary sense. As Ronald Baxter so aptly put it, "The word 'prophet' can have a secondary meaning—pale in the full light of the primary. In the past the prophecy of the prophet was new truth revealed. In the present the prophecy of the pastor/teacher is the revealed truth proclaimed."[1] Criswell said, "A preacher who gives forth the message of God in the wisdom and power of the Holy Spirit has the gift of prophecy."[2] The gift of prophecy in this secondary sense is the "fearless proclamation of the Word of God, expounded in the light of the contemporary situation. The prophet's concern is the application of God's Word to God's people. The prophet is an expository preacher of the Word of God."[3]

Those who say that the gift of prophecy is extant in a secondary sense must answer the question, How does an expository preacher of the Word of God differ from the expository teacher of the Word of God? The difference cannot be one of content, since both begin with the expositional study of the Word of God. Neither can the difference be one of delivery. A pastor who is gifted as a teacher and has good communication skills will be just as animated and excited in his delivery as the pastor who is gifted as a prophet. The difference between the prophet and the teacher must be one of motivation and emphasis. The teacher begins with a desire to expound the Word, while the prophet begins with a desire to expose sin and produce holiness. The contrast between the prophet and the teacher is shown in the chart at the end of this chapter.

What are the characteristics of a person possessing (in a secondary sense) this gift of prophecy? He will exhibit a fearless adherence to the truth of God's Word. He will be an outspoken, clear-cut crusader for the Word. He will emphasize the principles of the Word that produce holiness of life. He will see only black and white, and he will be quick to point out sin. His messages will be mostly topical, dealing with current, cutting issues. His preaching, whatever the type or style, will be heavy in the area of personal application. He will want the people to whom he preaches to apply Biblical truths to their daily lives. He will use the Word of God as a swift javelin whose point is honed to seek out sin.

Ed Miller, a very dear friend of mine now serving the Lord faithfully in Rhode Island, possesses these characteristics. Even his greeting carries a prod to godliness and holiness. Other brothers in Christ may say, "How's the Lord been treating you lately?" But Ed says, "How have you been treating the Lord lately?"

The result of the exercise of the gift of prophecy will be seen in the conviction of the hearers. They will be convinced that what they have heard is truth. The "thus saith the Lord" will have come through loud and clear to them. Their conviction will lead to conformity. The hearers will be convinced intellectually (comprehension); they will be convinced volitionally (conviction); they will be convinced that they must apply the truths they have heard to their lives (conformity). The result of the exercise of the gift of prophecy is not a tribute to the excellence of the preacher, but a testimony to the efficacy of the gift.

A prophet could exercise his gift as a pastor, itinerant evangelist, deeper-life speaker, or revival speaker. Someone who is not a fulltime Christian worker could exercise the gift of prophecy in a variety of ways. He could serve as a youth worker—his emphasis and motivation will be the personal holiness and sanctification of the youth under his care. He could teach a Sunday school class or lead a Bible study—in both cases his emphasis will be the fearless expounding of the Word that exposes sin. Whether or not a prophet has a particular job within the church, he will find it impossible to be silent and will speak out definitively and succinctly on contemporary issues. When he offers counsel, his emphasis will always be a no-nonsense call to godly living. Every church needs the exercise of the gift of prophecy as a checks-and-balance system against compromise.

SELF-EVALUATION

	Yes	No
1. Do I exhibit fearless adherence to the truth of God's Word?	❏	❏
2. Am I outspoken?	❏	❏
3. Are my thoughts clear-cut?	❏	❏
4. Am I decisive?	❏	❏
5. Do I motivate others to live holy lives?	❏	❏
6. Do I see only black and white?	❏	❏
7. When I explain a Scriptural truth, do others comprehend what God is saying?	❏	❏
8. When I explain a portion of Scripture, am I convinced that my interpretation is correct?	❏	❏
9. Does my life conform to the Biblical standard?	❏	❏

If most of your answers are yes, you may possess the gift of prophecy.

EVANGELISM

The gift of evangelism is certainly viable today, and very necessary. Our English word "evangelist/evangelize/evangelism" is really a transliteration of the Greek word, not a translation. The original Greek term is made up of two parts: a base word and a prefix. The base word is transliterated *angelos* and translated "messenger." The prefix *eu* means "well or good." Thus our English word means "messenger of good news/to proclaim the good news/proclamation of the good news." James Gray's definition is "to be a bringer of good tidings."[4]

There is a very close connection between the Greek verb *euangelizo* and the Hebrew word *bissar,* meaning "proclaim good news." *Euangelizo* is used in the Septuagint in a variety of contexts such as "bringing news of victory" and "political or private communications that bring joy."[5] Often it is used simply to denote "news bearer."[6]

The four Gospel writers are called evangelists because they proclaimed the good news. The Anglo-Saxons called the good news *God's spell* and this phrase became shortened with usage to "gospel." The gospel is literally the good news capsulized for us by Paul in 1 Corinthians 15:3-4: "That Christ died for our sins according to the Scriptures, and that He was buried, and that He rose again the third day according to the Scriptures." Evangelism then is the proclamation of Christ's vicarious atonement—vindicated by His resurrection and ascension—as the solution to man's sin problem. The evangelist is one who proclaims this message. Evangelism is more than just preaching/teaching; it is "proclaiming with full authority and power...It effects salvation."[7]

The work of evangelism was given to all the disciples and, by application, to us as well. We are required by Christ's command in Acts 1:8 and Matthew 28:19-20 to take the good news to every nation. We are required by moral obligation (the basic meaning of "debtor" in Romans 1:14) to share with unsaved mankind the forgiveness we have found in Christ. We are answerable to God for whether or not we share our faith with others (1 Corinthians 9:16). Paul exhorted Timothy in 2 Timothy 4:5

to "do the work of an evangelist." No one is exempt from sharing the good news. In our own way, as God provides opportunity, we should always be ready to give to every man who asks a reason for the hope that is in us (1 Peter 3:15). The work of evangelism is to be our constant desire and the aim of our life in Christ.

But beyond the *work* of evangelism is the *gift* of evangelism. As John Walvoord put it, "All are responsible to share....Timothy was told to 'do the work of an evangelist.'...Some men have a special gift to communicate the Gospel in a way in which men respond."[8] All are obligated to exercise the privilege and duty of evangelism, "but some are especially endued with [the gift]."[9]

The gift of evangelism can be defined as follows: It is the "unusual capacity to preach and win the lost to Christ";[10] "the ability to persuade people to receive Christ as personal Savior and become His disciples";[11] "the capacity to present the Gospel message with exceptional clarity and overwhelming burden";[12] a gift "given to certain men enduing them with extraordinary power in public address and in personal evangelism";[13] "the gift of proclaiming the Good News of salvation effectively so that people respond to the claims of Christ in conversion and in discipleship."[14] The key word in this last definition is *effectively*.

The result of the exercise of the gift of evangelism is that people respond in saving faith. Why is it that a Jack Wyrtzen or a Billy Graham can preach a simple message and people respond? Someone else could preach the same message word for word and nothing would happen. Is it the man? No. Is it his delivery? No. Is it the message? No. It is his gift of evangelism. Those without the gift still preach evangelistic messages. God blesses His Word and some respond. But the overwhelming response we see in a Billy Graham crusade, for example, is due to the exercise of the gift of evangelism. Through the ages individuals have possessed and exercised this gift. The Wesley brothers, George Whitefield, Billy Sunday, D. L. Moody, and Percy Crawford come to mind as examples of men who saw tremendous response to their presentation of the gospel.

Certainly not all who possess this gift are well-known evangelists. The only man called an evangelist in Scripture is Philip, a deacon in the early church (Acts 21:8). Today an army of men and women whose names are virtually unknown exercise this gift with great success through personal evangelism. Henry Clay Trumbull, Will H. Houghton, Walter Wilson, and William McCarrell were part of this army and hundreds follow in their train. God has placed people possessing the gift of evangelism in every church.

One of the greatest soul-winners I have ever known is a restaurant owner named Rich Scordato. Less than a year after his conversion he had led more than 80 percent of his staff to Christ. His life is dedicated to reaching the lost. God has given him a unique ability to make contact with people and win them for Christ.

There seems to be a logical order to the offices mentioned in Ephesians 4:11. The evangelists follow the apostles and prophets, but precede the pastors and teachers. Since the offices of apostle and prophet have ceased (see appendix A), the work of evangelism is preparatory for all else to take place. The evangelist "moves about in different localities proclaiming the Gospel to those who were ignorant of it before. As they are converted and united to Jesus Christ in saving faith, the work of the pastor/ teacher begins....The work and gift of evangelism form the vanguard of the Church, establishing a beachhead in the new frontier upon which a church can be built."[15]

What are the characteristics of a person possessing the gift of evangelism? Because of his burning desire for the salvation of the lost, the fulltime evangelist will have a tendency to be transient. "The evangelist has no fixed place of residence, but moves about in different localities."[16] Whether or not he is a fulltime Christian worker, he will have a consuming passion for souls.[17] This burden will push him to intercede in prayer for their salvation.[18] He will share the desire expressed by C. T. Studd (missionary to three continents):

> Some want to live within the sound
> Of Church or chapel bell;

> I want to run a rescue ship
> Within a yard of Hell.[19]

The person possessing this gift will witness frequently and be an active participant in the evangelistic ministries of his church.[20] His emphasis is almost always going to be unilateral: the lost.

SELF-EVALUATION

	Yes	No
1. Do I have a burning desire for the lost?	❑	❑
2. Do I witness frequently?	❑	❑
3. Do I want every sermon to be evangelistic?	❑	❑
4. Do I think there should be an altar call every Sunday?	❑	❑
5. Do I spend much time in prayer for the lost?	❑	❑
6. When I witness, are people convicted by the Holy Spirit?	❑	❑
7. Are people converted as a result of my testimony?	❑	❑

If most of your answers are yes, you may possess the gift of evangelism.

SHEPHERDING

The term *shepherd* is a very common word in both the Old and New Testaments. In several places God Himself is pictured as the Shepherd of Israel. Psalm 95:7 speaks of Israel (and us by application) as being "the people of His pasture, / And the sheep of His hand." Perhaps the clearest use of the metaphor is found in Psalm 23, where David began by saying, "Jehovah, my shepherd is" (my translation).

Jeremiah and Ezekiel used the term to refer to the religious leaders of Israel. These references were mostly negative, excoriating the leaders for their utter failure as shepherds. The promise announced by the prophets is that one day God will set up one shepherd over the people (Jeremiah 23:3; Ezekiel 37:24).

In the New Testament there is a Psalm 23 in the Gospel of John, where Jesus described Himself as the Good Shepherd. The "good" or real shepherd is the One who is willing to lay down His life on behalf of His sheep (John 10:11).

In 1 Peter 5:4 Peter referred to Jesus as the Chief Shepherd. Peter's use of "Chief" implies that there were undershepherds who, in this context, would be the elders of 5:1. The term "pastors" in Ephesians 4:11 must also refer to undershepherds.

What does the task of shepherding entail? The root word of "to shepherd" means "to pasture, to rule, to gather the dispersed, to care for the weak, to tend the flock and to protect them." It also has the connotation of "to lead, guide, and go before."[21] A beautiful picture of the task of the shepherd is painted for us in Psalm 23. The task can be summed up in two words: total care. David, who experienced this total care, said that because the Lord was his shepherd, want for him did not exist.

David went on to talk about areas encompassed by this "care package." In Psalm 23:2 he talked about *provision.* One of the most important responsibilities of the shepherd is to provide food for the sheep. The term translated "green pastures" literally means "pastures of tender green shoots." The true shepherd is not satisfied just to find food; he searches for the very best food for his flock. In John 21 (KJV), three times the risen Christ instructed Peter to feed His sheep. Peter passed the message on to the elders when he exhorted them to "feed the flock of God" (1 Peter 5:2, KJV). Since the primary function of the shepherd is feeding, the bulk of a shepherd's time must be spent in study so that he can continually feed the flock. Since the shepherd is the one who leads his sheep to pasture, he must know where the good food is.

In Psalm 23:3 David spoke about *production.* David left the imagery of the shepherd for a moment and in straightforward prose stated, "He leads me in the paths of righteousness." This verse reminds us of the words of the apostle John: "I have no greater joy than to hear that my children walk in truth" (3 John 4). Likewise Paul's goal was "that [I] may present every man perfect [mature] in Christ Jesus" (Colossians 1:28). Paul could consider his ministry completed only when those under his care had reached maturity in Christ. The shepherd tends the sheep so that they will progress in godliness.

In Psalm 23:4 David spoke of the *protection* of rod and staff. The shepherd's crooked staff is used to extricate wandering sheep from thorns or other precarious situations. The shepherd's rod is used as a club for driving off wild animals. As Leslie Flynn put it, the shepherd's threefold responsibility is to guide, graze, and guard.[22]

Understanding Psalm 23 makes defining the gift of shepherding fairly easy. Charles Ryrie defined the possessor of this gift as "one who leads, provides, cares for, and protects the flock."[23] John Walvoord said, "The first work of the pastor is to feed the flock."[24] Packo defined the gift as the "ability to care for, protect from error, and feed a group of believers with the Word of God."[25] The responsibility of the person possessing the gift of shepherding is to "feed, protect, disciple, and equip the sheep. [The possessor] expresses an understanding, and sensitivity with regard to the needs of God's children."[26] Peter Wagner said, "The gift of pastoring is the special ability that God gives to certain members of the Body of Christ to assume a long-term personal responsibility for the spiritual welfare of a group of believers."[27]

The gift of shepherding begins with God giving a person a burden for the spiritual welfare of a particular group of God's people. The burden then motivates the person to take on the responsibility of a shepherd. He will assume all of the characteristics of a shepherd and perform all the tasks in the job description in Psalm 23. His work will not be complete until all of the sheep under his care reach maturity in Christ. Perhaps the gift could be described as "spiritual mothering."

A person possessing this gift will have a shepherd's heart. This inherent part of the gift cannot be manufactured, acquired, or learned. The true shepherd in John 10 had a shepherd's heart. The hireling did not. The true shepherd has genuine concern for the sheep because they are *his* sheep. The person with this gift has a feeling of possessing the people under his care. He often uses the personal pronoun *my*.

The shepherd's commitment is long-term[28] because his goal is to lead each sheep to maturity in Christ. Because he cares about his group and is committed to it, he is able to solve problems between people in the group.[29]

The gift of shepherding is not only given to those who are vocationally ministers.[30] A Sunday school teacher, youth worker, discussion leader, or home Bible study leader may possess this gift. Someone possessing this gift could easily find himself serving in a variety of roles. He could serve as a counselor or assume responsibility for the spiritual development of one person or a small group in a discipleship ministry. Older women with this gift could find themselves shepherding and training younger women. In one church a lady named Betty Davis had a tremendous ministry among young mothers. She shepherded her little flock and produced maturity in their lives. Any church could use many people with this gift to nurture and develop those who are young in the faith.

The gift of shepherding is verifiable through results. People who are shepherded will be edified and they will evidence measurable progress toward maturity. The "sheep" will have an unswerving confidence in their shepherd and will open up to him so that he will have tremendous opportunities for input, direction, and the application of the Word to the problems in their lives. And the sheep will know that they are being fed. A person with this gift will have a difficult time sitting in a class; the gift requires an outlet and the shepherd will want to teach the sheep.

SELF-EVALUATION

	Yes	No
1. Do I feel genuine concern for a flock?	❏	❏

	Yes	No
2. Do I speak of a group as *"my* group"?	❏	❏
3. Have I made a long-term commitment to my group?	❏	❏
4. Is my goal to bring members of my group to maturity in Christ?	❏	❏
5. Am I able to solve problems between people?	❏	❏
6. Do I require an outlet?	❏	❏
7. Does my activity result in edification?	❏	❏
8. Do I see in my group measurable progress toward maturity?	❏	❏
9. Do members of my group have unswerving confidence in me?	❏	❏
10. Do members of my group know they are being fed?	❏	❏

If most of your answers are yes, you may possess the gift of shepherding.

TEACHING

The gift of teaching is basic and its exercise is absolutely necessary if the church of Jesus Christ is to survive in this generation and continue into the next.

The root word translated "teach/teacher/teaching" is *didasko.* It "denotes teaching, instruction in the widest sense....The aim is the highest possible development of the talents of the pupil....To teach always involves an adverb—successfully."[31] The gift of teaching is the ability to "expound the Scriptures. It is the most important function of the body of Christ. The gift is one of communication, not superior knowledge; it is the capacity for successful communication and application of truth to another individual."[32] Most other definitions feature the words *explain* and *apply.* "It is the ability to explain and apply Christian doctrine."[33] "It is the ability to communicate the Word of

God by explaining and applying truth."[34] "[It is] the supernatural ability to explain and apply truths which have already been received by the Church."[35]

The gift of teaching includes the divinely bestowed ability to organize truth and lucidly communicate God's Word. The sign on the teacher's desk might read, "God's Word Made Plain." Making God's Word plain is what the teacher does best. When one who possesses the gift of teaching finishes the lesson, those who have heard it know what God's Word says.

These definitions tell us there is a distinct difference between the gift of teaching and those gifts that are revelatory in character. The revelatory gifts deal with new truth being received; teaching involves expounding truth already delivered. "As distinct from the ecstatic exhortation of prophets, the instruction given by teachers would be exposition of the Old Testament and of the words and acts of Christ."[36] "The prophetic gift was sporadic, that of teaching was continuous; the former came by momentary inspiration, the latter was the outcome of long experience."[37]

The importance of the gift of teaching was underscored by Leslie Flynn as he related it to the body of truth referred to by Jude as "the faith." This body of truth has been propagated, protected, preserved, and proclaimed for almost two thousand years chiefly through the exercise of the gift of teaching. Exhortations to teach, learn, grow in knowledge and understanding, study, and come to the knowledge of the truth are legion in Scripture.

The Word of God is depicted as food necessary to the growth of the believer (1 Peter 2:2). The Word is the vehicle used by the Holy Spirit to produce holiness in the life (John 17:17). The Word is pictured by Paul as our offensive weaponry (Ephesians 6:17). The Word is to be the object of constant study (1 Timothy 4:13). For almost two thousand years the gift of teaching has been the vehicle God has used to explain His Word.

There is a difference between being apt to teach and possessing the gift of teaching. The word "apt" means "a capacity for, potential for, disposal to, readiness for, fitness for, suitability to, inclination to."[38] In Scripture the word translated "apt to teach" or "able to teach" is *didaktikos*. *Didaktikos* is only used in two verses: in 1 Timothy 3:2 as one of the qualifications for a bishop; and in 2 Timothy 2:24 as part of the description of the servant of God. Arndt and Gingrich rendered *didaktikos* as "skillful in teaching."[39] Rengstorf defined it as "able to teach."[40] Those who are apt to teach do not necessarily possess the gift of teaching, but are seasoned enough in the Word to instruct others.

The results of the exercise of the gift of teaching will be seen in the students. In the words of Peter Wagner, "This gift [teaching] has a built-in effectiveness—others will learn!"[41] When this gift is being used, communication takes place at a very high level. The teacher's God-given capacity to communicate Biblical truth clearly will elicit (audibly or inaudibly) this reaction from his students: "I see what he means."[42]

A person possessing the gift of teaching will exhibit certain telltale characteristics. Packo listed six: (1) he will analyze and systematize Biblical knowledge; (2) he will engage in research in order to prove Biblical truth; (3) he will be able to explain truth clearly; (4) he will usually produce more material than he can ever cover in a one-hour class; (5) he will spend time in word studies to assure accuracy in his statements; (6) his ministry results in learning.[43] McRae said a person with this gift "will engage with high interest in personal Bible study; he will pursue language study, hermeneutics, Bible study methods; he will spend time studying history and geography as well as theology."[44] The result of these characteristics is clear communication that explains and opens up Bible truth.

One man with the gift of teaching was Dr. Charles Woodbridge, who for many years was the featured teacher for Word of Life. Other men with the gift whom I have been privileged to hear are Dr. John Whitcomb of Grace Seminary, Dr. Lehman Strauss, the Reverend William Harding, and Dr. Charles Anderson. Fred Rodtnick and Louis Clifford are laymen endowed by God with the gift of teaching.

The gift of teaching is particularly important and the need for its exercise continues today. The last office in Ephesians 4:11, the pastor/teacher is the one who is there for the long haul to train and equip the saints.

SELF-EVALUATION

	Yes	No
1. Do I analyze and systematize Biblical truth?	❏	❏
2. Do I engage in research to prove truth?	❏	❏
3. Do I produce more material than I can ever cover?	❏	❏
4. Do I spend time in word studies to ensure the accuracy of my material?	❏	❏
5. Do I organize my material?	❏	❏
6. When I teach, do others learn?	❏	❏
7. When I teach, do students say, "I see what he means"?	❏	❏
8. Do I see measurable progress in the maturity of my students?	❏	❏
9. Do my students increase their knowledge of the Bible?	❏	❏

If most of your answers are yes, you may possess the gift of teaching.

So far we have discussed the gifts of pastoring (shepherding) and teaching separately—and they do exist independently of each other. But because Paul listed pastors and teachers together in Ephesians 4:11, we should take the time to consider them in this context as well.[45]

Anyone assuming primary pastoral responsibilities in a local church should possess both the gift of shepherding and the gift of teaching. Speaking of the link between these two gifts in the office of pastor/teacher, John Walvoord said, "The true shepherd must be able to feed his flock."[46] Packo said that the one fulfilling the office of shepherding "will also have the teaching gift."[47] McRae said, "There are two distinct dimensions. As pastor, he has the capacity to 'shepherd'; as teacher he has the ability to prepare and serve a balanced diet that is nutritious spiritually...[that will] produce growth in the people."[48] Charles Ryrie commented concerning the gift of teaching: "It can be given alone, or in conjunction with the gift of pastoring."[49]

Let me emphasize the distinction between the gifts of pastoring and teaching and the office of pastor/teacher. Some people with the gift of teaching do not have the gift of pastoring, and some people with the gift of pastoring do not have the gift of teaching, but anyone fulfilling the *office* of pastor/teacher must possess both gifts.[50] The gift of shepherding will give him a loving, caring heart for people, and the gift of teaching will enable him to feed his flock. Both gifts are essential to the combined office.

Sometimes pastors of large churches have the gift of faith or leadership rather than the gifts of shepherding and teaching. Such leaders must surround themselves with those who possess the gifts of shepherding and teaching if the ministries of their churches are to be productive.

In my experience the call of God to the ministry is punctuated by the emergence of the gift of shepherding manifested in an overwhelming burden to care for people spiritually. The sine qua non of the ministry is a shepherd's heart. A person who is a teacher par excellence but does not possess a shepherd's heart will be misplaced in the office of pastor/teacher. The position should be filled only by one who is specially called by God. It is neither an elected office nor a selected one. It is not a profession as much as it is an obsession.

EXHORTATION

There is an inseparable link between all spiritual gifts and the work of the Holy Spirit, but there is a sense in which the gift of exhortation has an even closer bond with the Spirit. The word Paul used in Romans 12:8 to refer to this gift *(parakaleo)* comes from the same root as the word John used in John 14 to refer to the Holy Spirit, our Paraclete. The ministry of an exhorter will bear a likeness to the ministry of the Holy Spirit in the life of a believer. As we study the definition of *parakaleo,* we can think

of both the spiritual gift of exhortation and the work of the Holy
Spirit of God in the lives of believers.

Parakaleo is a compound word consisting of a preposition
meaning "alongside or beside" and a verb meaning "to call."
Etymologically *para-kaleo* means "to call alongside in the sense
of summoning for assistance."[51] Thus the Comforter in John 14
is the One called alongside to help bear a burden or to assist—a
great description of the work of the blessed Holy Spirit in the
life of every believer.

Parakaleo has a variety of meanings, depending on the context. The word can mean "to call to one's aid, to call upon for
help, appeal to, urge, exhort, encourage, request, implore, entreat, comfort, cheer up, or console."[52] It can have the connotation of "admonish, enjoin, urgently impress on."[53] "When it
means 'comfort, consolation,' there is always the underlying
note of encouragement."[54] It can be a "word of encouragement,"
a pep talk, if you will, by a leader before a battle.[55] It can mean
"comfort" in the sense of "speaking to the heart."[56] In a negative context it can mean "seduce or entice."[57]

These meanings of *parakaleo* can help us understand the gift
of exhortation. Charles Ryrie defined this gift as "the God-given
ability to encourage, comfort, admonish, and entreat."[58] Peter
Wagner stated that the gift is "the special ability God gives certain members of the Body of Christ to minister words of comfort, consolation, encouragement, and counsel to other members of the Body in such a way that they feel helped and com-
forted."[59] John Packo said, "It is the Spirit-given ability to encourage and counsel a believer in his/her faith so that the believer experiences comfort and guidance."[60]

If the gift of exhortation is being exercised, certain results
will be seen in the lives of the hearers. The measurement of
these results, however, is subjective at best. Thinking of the results, McQuay said that exhortation is "the Divine enablement
to comfort, strengthen, and disciple another so that he/she is
stimulated to action."[61] Another writer defined the gift as "the
ability to motivate people through encouraging words to live
practical Christian lives."[62]

The exhorter is a problem-solver. He has the ability to see

the root of a problem and prescribe a series of steps for solving it. The exercise of his gift produces cheer and encouragement. His gift is the God-given ability to "dispel grief by the imputation of strength."[63] The exhorter expresses his gift in a variety of ways including "personal presence...visits of sympathy... joining in lamenting and sorrowing, or a letter of condolence."[64] One of the best Scriptural examples of how this gift operates through an individual is seen in Barnabas. He so epitomized the exhorter that he was called the "son of consolation" (Acts 4:36, KJV).

The gift of exhortation provides keen insight into people and their needs, and prompts just the right actions or words to encourage people. This gift uses the vehicles of speech and communication, but it differs from other speaking gifts in that its primary targets are individuals rather than groups of people. As Peter Wagner said, "Exhortation is a special gift for Christian counseling."[65] A person with this gift will draw people like a magnet. They will be attracted because of the compassion they sense and the profound help they receive.

I am reminded of Doris, the wife of a very dear pastor friend of mine. My first impression was that she had an unusual ability to read people. Then I discovered that she had an unusual ability to read situations. Next I discovered that she had an unusual ability to break down a complex situation, get to the heart of the problem, and give encouragement, comfort, and advice that would lead to solving the problem. She has the gift of exhortation and what a blessing the exercise of this gift is to the body of Christ!

John Packo must have had someone like Doris in mind when he listed five characteristics of a person possessing this gift:[66] (1) he encourages believers who are discouraged; (2) he goes out of his way to cheer people; (3) he counsels believers with the Word; (4) he is able to guide people through their difficulties; (5) he is a person in whom others readily confide.

Our own daughter Dawn also possesses this gift. She attracts people with problems as an oasis attracts weary travelers. Even people who are older than she is readily confide in her. Dawn is motivated by the stress and heartache of others. Her little notes of encouragement to me adorn the paneled walls of my study as a constant reminder to me of the Barnabas God has placed within our family.

SELF-EVALUATION

	Yes	No
1. Am I need-motivated?	❑	❑
2. Am I able to sense needs in the body?	❑	❑
3. Do I relate to people best one-on-one?	❑	❑
4. Do I emphasize the application of truth?	❑	❑
5. Am I able to size up situations, draw conclusions, and then act on the basis of those conclusions?	❑	❑
6. Are people comforted and encouraged after talking to me?	❑	❑
7. Are people motivated to action as a result of talking to me?	❑	❑
8. If I make a suggestion to someone, does he respond, "I'll do that"?	❑	❑
9. Do people find my counsel valid?	❑	❑

If most of your answers are yes, you may possess the gift of exhortation.

Have you spotted yourself yet in any of these descriptions of people possessing speaking gifts? Do any of these gifts seem to be yours? Put a mental check mark beside the ones that do. Also make a mental note of the gifts that definitely are not yours. This self-evaluation may help narrow the field as you try to pinpoint your spiritual gifts.

SPEAKING GIFTS COMPARED

	PROPHET	EVANGELIST	PASTOR	TEACHER	EXHORTER
MOTIVATION	Exposure of sin	Condition of the lost	Burden to care for a particular part of God's flock	Exposition of Scripture	Needs of the individual
EMPHASIS	Holiness of life	God's saving grace in redemption	Spiritual nurture and growth	Organization of material	Application of material
AUDIENCE	Class or individual	The lost—ones, twos, or a crowd	Group as opposed to an individual	Class more often than individual	Individual more often than group
TOOL	Ability to cut through externals and touch the heart and conscience	Ability to communicate convincingly	Ability to feed, counsel, and care for the flock	Ability to exegete Scripture	Great ability to sense real needs
RESULTS	People are convicted of sin and live sanctified lives.	People respond in saving faith.	The sheep grow.	The body is edified.	The body is edified.

5

SERVING GIFTS

Serving gifts include faith, helps, giving, administration, and mercy. J. I. Packer called them "Samaritan Gifts—loving, helpful responses to others' physical and material needs."[1]

FAITH

The spiritual gift of faith is not *saving* faith. Every believer in Jesus Christ is part of God's redeemed family because he responded to the claims of Christ in saving faith. Paul said in Ephesians 2:8, "By grace you have been saved through faith."

Neither is this gift *living* faith. Habakkuk 2:4 says, "The just shall live by his faith." This verse was quoted twice by Paul and once by the author of Hebrews (Romans 1:17; Galatians 3:11; Hebrews 10:38). The writer of Hebrews also reminded us in 11:6 that "without faith it is impossible to please Him." The believer saved by faith must continue to live by faith. Second Corinthians 5:7 says, "We walk by faith, not by sight." Life in Christ is a life lived by faith.

Life in Christ is begun by saving faith and is continued by living faith. But beyond both of these spheres is the spiritual gift of faith. Perhaps this gift is that mountain-moving faith of which Jesus spoke: "If you have faith as a mustard seed..." (Matthew 17:20). Certain believers in the body of Christ have received from God the Holy Spirit a seemingly boundless reservoir of faith called the gift of faith. "The gift of faith is different from other types of faith. It is special faith that supernaturally achieves what is impossible through human instrumentality."[2]

Several authors link the gift of faith to miracles and define it as miracle-working faith. For example Paul Zehr wrote, "The gift of faith is a wonder-working faith manifesting itself in works rather than words, and evidencing itself in healings and miracles."[3] Palma defined the gift as "an endowment of the Holy Spirit that enables a person to believe for and expect extraordinary demonstrations of the power of God—i.e. miracles."[4] Certainly faith was required by the individuals performing miracles in the first century, but there is no Scriptural link between the gift of faith (which is active today) and the gift of miracles (which is not extant). The fact that Paul listed faith separately from miracles (1 Corinthians 12:9-10) would tend to indicate a much wider application of the gift of faith.

Other authors see the gift of faith as a fire alarm box with a sign stating, "Break glass only in case of fire." Carlson defined the gift as "mountain-moving faith...that is given in an emergency or moment of extreme need."[5] But if we remember that spiritual gifts are sovereignly dispensed once for all by the Holy Spirit of God, we realize that Carlson's concept is not valid. Certainly God is able to do anything and He could easily supply great faith in an emergency, but such faith is not the spiritual gift of faith.

Charles Ryrie defined the gift as "the God-given ability for the believer to trust in God's power to supply and guide."[6] McQuay wrote that the gift of faith is "the ability to see something that needs to be done, to believe God wants to do it, and will do it. It usually is prompted by special needs above the ordinary circumstances we face every day in our lives."[7] Other definitions are similar: "It is the capacity to see something that needs to be done and believe God will do it through him, even though it looks impossible."[8] "It is the ability to recognize what God wants to do in a seemingly impossible situation and trust God will get the work accomplished. It disregards insurmountable obstacles and claims the answer."[9]

A person with the gift of faith will have vision when others have none; he will believe God for the supplying of needs in a supernatural way.[10] In the face of the impossible, he will have an unshakable conviction that God will bring it to pass.[11] Down through the ages the church of Jesus Christ has been blessed, edified, and challenged by men possessing the grand gift of faith.

George Muller comes immediately to mind. God used his gift of faith to supply the needs of his orphanage housing two thousand orphans in Bristol, England. The stories concerning his prayers and God's answers are living testimony to what the exercise of this gift can accomplish. (See appendix B regarding intercession and the gift of faith.)

A man in our generation with the same gift is Jack Wyrtzen, founder of Word of Life. In the beginning Jack and Harry Bollback trusted God for the money needed to purchase an island in the center of Schroon Lake and the years have borne testimony to their vision and faith. God's phenomenal blessings in response to that faith have been seen as Word of Life has grown by leaps and bounds in the United States and expanded to Europe, South America, and Africa. Each day money to sustain the work is literally "prayed in."

A person with the gift of faith is more interested in the future than in history. He is goal-centered, a possibility-thinker, a dreamer. Believers with this gift have altered the course of history and have been the agents through whom great leaps forward have been achieved by the church.

Self-Evaluation

	Yes	No
1. Do I have vision when others don't?	❑	❑
2. Do I believe God will supply needs in a supernatural way?	❑	❑
3. Do I have unshakable conviction in the face of impossible odds?	❑	❑
4. Am I more interested in the future than the past?	❑	❑
5. Am I goal-centered?	❑	❑
6. Do I focus on the possibilities rather than the problems of a situation?	❑	❑
7. Is my faith rewarded by answers to prayer?	❑	❑

	Yes	No
8. Am I able to trust God for the impossible?	❏	❏
9. Do I press toward my goal with confidence, ignoring distractions?	❏	❏

If most of your answers are yes, you may possess the gift of faith.

HELPS/MINISTERING (SERVING)

The words *helps* and *ministering (serving)* seem to refer to the same gift. This is one of the most widely held and one of the more diversified of the gifts.

The term translated "helps" in 1 Corinthians 12:28 *(antilempsis)* is a hopoxlegomena, only occurring here in the New Testament. The term translated "helps" in Acts 27:17 (KJV) is *boetheia*, which is not even remotely related to *antilempsis*. Sumrall said the "helps" in Acts 27:17 "were rope-like cables used to wrap around a ship during a storm [to help hold her together]."[12] These cables, though obviously not the gift of helps, are a good illustration of the function of the spiritual gift.

Antilempsis comes from the verb form *antilambano,* which is used in three passages in the New Testament (Luke 1:54; Acts 20:35; 1 Timothy 6:2). The basic meaning of the verb is to "help, take someone's part, come to the aid of, take part in, devote oneself to."[13] *Antilambano* is a compound word made up of a preposition *(anti)* meaning "opposite, against, in the place of" and a verb *(lambano)* meaning "to take or receive." It is easy to see how the word translates into "help, aid."

Griffiths said that the gift of helps involves "helping the needy, sick, and weak—the kind of work for which the deacons were first appointed."[14] The deacons did care for the physical needs of the neglected widows, but the main purpose of the selection of deacons was to free up the apostolate to perform their tasks of study, prayer, and leadership.

John Packo defined the gift of helps as "the Spirit-given ability to give practical assistance that encourages other believers to fulfill their responsibilities. It is any discharge of service given in genuine love lending assistance that results in freeing up others for using their gifts in ministry."[15] Wagner also tied the exercise of this gift to the freeing up of other Christians to exercise their particular gifts.[16] Leslie Flynn said, "The gift of helps is the Spirit-given ability to serve the Church in any supporting role....Those served then have more time and energy for the ministry of prayer and preaching, resulting in blessing to others....This gift is not for helping the poor, sick, aged, orphans, and widows [which is really the gift of mercy], but for lending a hand wherever it will release other workers for their spiritual ministries."[17]

The term translated "ministering" (Romans 12:7) and transliterated *diakonia* is the root of our English word "deacon." Thus the gift of ministering (serving) became personified in the office of deacon. Originally *diakonia* meant "to wait on tables," but grew to embrace the broader meaning of "to provide or care for, to serve [as a comprehensive term] in the sense of to organize, disperse, and oversee meals."[18] "Jesus used the term to refer to the full sum of active Christian love for the neighbor, and as such it is a mark of true discipleship."[19] Generally the word came to be applied to all significant activity for the edification of the Christian community. Paul used the term to mean "to wait on someone, serve, care for, take care of, look after, help, support, aid."[20] Such service "is helping in the broadest sense. It includes ministering to the physical and bodily needs of others."[21]

The relationship between *antilempsis* and *diakonia* is well-stated by Kittel: "In general, the 'helps' mentioned in 1 Corinthians 12:28 must have formed the content of these acts of service, namely acts of care and assistance on behalf of the community."[22]

According to John Walvoord the gift of helps may come closest to "universal possession [by the church]. The dimensions are many and differ with the individual enabling him to minister in different ways—without the operation of this gift, the task of the Church would be impossible."[23] Peter Wagner said that this gift is "task-oriented. It is usually directed more to an institution than the individual."[24] The motivation of a person possessing this gift is to free up others so that they can use their gifts. The expression of the gift of helps is "broad-based service in general including all good works that promote and edify the Body of Christ. A person possessing this gift is ready and willing to fit in anywhere with a joyous spirit of service."[25] This gift is "seen most visibly in those who place themselves at the disposal of others."[26] Unlike some of the other gifts that translate into a particular skill, the "skill" or ability par excellence of the person with the gift of helps is availability! He may have a variety of talents, and so he takes upon himself a variety of tasks to free up others to use their gifts. (See appendix B regarding hospitality and the gift of serving.)

One lady I know who possesses the gift of helps is Emma Hill. When my wife and I were in our first pastorate—we were young and limited somewhat by our first child and a small income—Emma volunteered her services as a baby sitter for any time or any occasion, personal or business, and would not accept a penny for her work. In fact she always left something more than sweetener in our sugar bowl. Her reason for volunteering was simple and very Scriptural: "I really feel that my ministry is to serve you and help you (to free you up) so that you can do your job of ministering." I am not sure Emma had any specialized training in understanding spiritual gifts, but she knew that her gift was serving and she received joy from using it.

People possessing the gift of helps have some characteristics in common: They usually avoid the limelight, but are part of the backbone of any effective church. They are jobbers in the sense of committing themselves to help people on short-term assignments. They would much rather assist a leader than be one. They are among the first to volunteer for any manual tasks around the church.[27]

The Scriptures record the names of many who used the gift of helps faithfully for the edification of the body of Christ. John Mark began his service for Christ in the capacity of helper. We are told in Acts 13:5 that as Paul and Barnabas left on their first

missionary journey they had John Mark as their "assistant." He
accompanied them with the intention of doing a variety of jobs
so that Paul and Barnabas could concentrate on their missionary
endeavors. Some of the other people included in the "Service
Hall of Fame" are listed at the end of Paul's Epistles to the Romans and Colossians. Most of these individuals would have re-
mained nameless and unknown (by personal choice) had it not
been for Paul. They represent a veritable army of other helpers
who through the ages have made a healthy church possible.

Listen to some of the names. "I commend to you Phoebe...a
servant of the church in Cenchrea....She has been a helper of
many and of myself also" (Romans 16:1-2). "Greet Priscilla and
Aquila, my fellow workers [helpers, KJV] in Christ Jesus" (16:3).
"Greet Mary, who labored much for us" (16:6). "Greet Urbanus,
our fellow worker [helper, KJV] in Christ" (16:9). "Greet
Tryphena and Tryphosa, who have labored in the Lord" (16:12).
"Greet the beloved Persis, who labored much in the Lord"
(16:12). "Tychicus...faithful minister, and fellow servant" (Colossians 4:7). "Aristarchus...Mark...Justus...fellow workers...
they have proved to be a comfort to me" (4:10-11). "Epaphras...a
bondservant of Christ...laboring fervently for you" (4:12).
"Archippus, 'Take heed to the ministry which you have received'" (4:17).

Some of the names in this list are immediately recognizable,
but most of them belong to behind-the-scenes workers who used
their gift of serving to free up others to use their gifts. Paul considered the ministry of these helpers vital. Without the gift of
helps, the church cannot function as it should. This gift is just as
necessary and valuable as other spiritual gifts.

If the church of Jesus Christ is compared to a finely tuned
Swiss watch, the members who have the gift of helps are the
jewels. Each jewel functions as a bearing, placed at a pivotal
point of stress because of its durability. Nothing runs more
smoothly than a fine watch with jeweled movement, and nothing runs more smoothly than the body of Christ when those with
the gift of helps are placed at the pivotal points of stress and
constant wear so that the other members are free to do their
respective tasks.

SELF-EVALUATION

	Yes	No
1. Am I motivated by a desire to free up others?	❏	❏
2. Am I willing to fit in anywhere?	❏	❏
3. Is my greatest ability availability?	❏	❏
4. Do I avoid the limelight?	❏	❏
5. Do I prefer short-term assignments?	❏	❏
6. As a result of my service does my church operate more smoothly?	❏	❏
7. As a result of my service are my church leaders more productive?	❏	❏
8. As a result of my service do other people in my church have more time to exercise their own gifts?	❏	❏

If most of your answers are yes, you may possess the gift of helps.

GIVING

Giving is a responsibility and obligation of worship laid on every child of God (1 Corinthians 16:2). But beyond that universal responsibility, there is a very special spiritual gift called the gift of giving.

What is the gift of giving? "The gift of Giving is that special ability that God gives to certain members of the Body of Christ to contribute their material resources to the work of the Lord with liberality and cheerfulness."[28] "The gift of Giving is the distribution of one's monies to others. It is done with simplicity—no thought of anything in return."[29] "It is the ability to earn and contribute an extraordinary proportion of income to the Lord's work."[30] The gift of giving is the "Spirit-given ability to share generously and cheerfully to further the work of God."[31] "It is the capacity to give of one's substance to the work of the Lord or to the people of God consistently, liberally, sacrificially, with wisdom and cheerfulness so that others experience blessing."[32] The gift of giving is "the ability to support the Lord's work materially with generous, timely, and cheerful contributions."[33]

Paul spoke of this gift in Romans 12:8. In this verse the word translated "liberality" or "simplicity" is *haplotes*. The term means "simplicity, sincerity, uprightness, frankness, generosity, liberality, single, simple, guileless."[34] It also carries the connotation of "open, without ulterior motive, unambiguously, wholeheartedly, innocent, pure, singleness of heart, sufficiency which has something to spare for others, generosity."[35] The verb form, *haploo,* literally means "to make single or unfold."[36] The literal meaning of the noun would refer to a piece of cloth that was unfolded and thus made into a single layer. Since it is impossible to hide anything in a piece of cloth that has been totally unfolded and laid out, *haplotes* came to mean "something completely open, that which has nothing hidden, the absence of any ulterior motives, that which is done openly for all to see."

When we apply these definitions to what Paul said about the gift of giving, Romans 12:8 becomes very clear. Paul was admonishing the giver to be motivated only by the desire and the ability to give. Paul's admonition reminds me of what Jesus said about the Pharisees, the hypocrites of His day. He charged them in Matthew 6:2 with sounding a trumpet when they gave alms and in 6:5 of praying loudly on street corners to be seen and heard of men. He ended both charges with the same phrase: "Assuredly, I say to you, they have their reward."

I am reminded again that God's concern, even in the Old Testament, was not for the offering, but for the heart of the offerer. God measures not the amount of the gift, but the attitude of the giver (see Mark 12:41-44). The most expensive gift in the world, given with wrong motives, is valueless as a means of seeking God's favor.

A person with the gift of giving will be motivated by the temporal needs of others and will respond through the exercise of this gift.[37] The person possessing this gift will respond more than just materially. This gift will produce in the possessor an attitude that makes his home a rent-free motel, his table a fine restaurant with no tab, his car a community bus that never seems to need gas, his schedule always flexible enough to care for needs of others, and anything he possesses a product of joint owner-ship (belonging to him and anyone else who needs it). (See appendix B regarding hospitality, voluntary poverty, and the gift of giving.)

People with the gift of giving will be magnanimous like Barnabas (Acts 4:32-37). He was motivated by the needs of others and he responded by selling land and giving the money to meet the needs of the saints in Jerusalem. His gift was straight-forward with no strings attached. He expected no brass band or service plaque, but experienced the joy of knowing he had a share in meeting needs. In contrast to Barnabas, Ananias and Sapphira wanted the praise of man for their great generosity (Acts 5:1-11). They may have given more money than Barnabas did, but God's reaction showed that it is not the amount of the gift but the attitude of the giver that matters to Him.

Barnabas reminds me of a deacon named Casey. Casey never buys one of anything. His immediate family consists of him and his wife, but at Thanksgiving he purchases enough turkeys to feed a troop. Today he and his wife are retired but working harder now than ever. They are involved in the perfect ministry for them: Operation Blessing, an organization God uses to provide food to those in need. Casey was never any happier than he is now. Why? Because he is working within the sphere of his spiritual gift of giving. And lives have been transformed because of the exercise of this man's spiritual gift.

SELF-EVALUATION

	Yes	No
1. Am I motivated by the temporal needs of others?	❑	❑
2. Do I give myself and my possessions as well as my money?	❑	❑

	Yes	No
3. Do I have a lot of money?	❏	❏
4. As a result of my giving, do people realize their needs are being met?	❏	❏
5. Does my giving contribute to a feeling of oneness, family, and caring in my church?	❏	❏
6. Does my giving spur others to give also?	❏	❏

If most of your answers are yes, you may possess the gift of giving.

ADMINISTRATION/LEADERSHIP

The terms *government* and *administration* deal with the same entity: leadership. The church has been blessed over the centuries with many possessing the gift of leadership, and in our generation Dr. Charles Stanley and the Reverend Jerry Falwell are good examples. The claim that certain people possess the gift is proven, in part, by the number of those who follow them.

Paul used two words to designate the gift of leadership. The first term, found in Romans 12:8, is translated "leads." The original word is a form of *proistemi,* which is a combination of *pro* ("before") and *histemi* ("to stand before"). *Proistemi* has a variety of meanings and connotations including "to put before; to preside; to lead, guide, direct, govern; to assist; to join with; to protect; to care for, to help, to further; to lead."[38] Reicke summed up these definitions by saying that the "primary task of [those possessing] this gift is caring for others."[39] (Paul used the same word in 1 Timothy 3:4-5 as he listed the leadership qualities necessary for the office of bishop.)

The second term, found in 1 Corinthians 12:28, is *kubernesis,* which is translated "administrations." The verb form *(kuberneo)* means "to steer a ship, or to act as a helmsman."[40] Put simply, the person possessing the gift of leadership possesses the gift of management.[41]

The writer of Hebrews used another term that contributes to our understanding of the gift of leadership. In Hebrews 13:7,17, 24 the word is translated "those who rule over you." Believers are admonished to remember their church leaders in prayer and as a pattern for godly living; to obey them and submit to their authority; and to greet them. The original word is a form of the verb *egeomai,* used to "denote non-Christian leaders, great men, officials, and priests; military leaders; leaders in the Church."[42] This verb may be taken from and be a close relative of *ago,* the very general Greek word meaning "to lead, guide."[43]

Considered together, the words in Romans 12:8, 1 Corinthians 12:28, and Hebrews 13:7,17,24 give us a full-orbed view of what the gift of leadership encompasses.

Various definitions add to our understanding: The gift of leadership is the "ability to rule in the Church."[44] This gift is "guiding or governing others including the ability to organize."[45] "It is the ability to guide or pilot. It offers direction in practical affairs of the Church in administrative matters."[46] "It is the Spirit-given ability to lead others by example and guide members of the Body to attain goals that glorify God."[47] "It is related to wise direction for the work of God....Those who lack the gift should seek counsel of those who [have it]."[48] "It is the Spirit-given ability that enables one to understand clearly the immediate and long range goals of a particular part of the Body of Christ, and to devise and execute effective plans for accomplishing those goals."[49] "It is the capacity to organize and administrate with such efficiency...that not only is the project completed, but done also harmoniously [with the result being] obvious blessing."[50]

All of these definitions give us basically the same picture. A person with the gift of leadership will have the ability to see and set needed goals, devise a plan to achieve those goals, and then motivate people to implement the plan. One of his outstanding characteristics will be the ability to organize and delegate.

According to John Packo, people possessing this gift exhibit the following characteristics: (1) They assume leadership responsibilities when there is an apparent lack of leadership. (2) They organize and motivate other believers to do the Lord's work. (3) They have the ability to organize people and programs to achieve goals. (4) They feel comfortable serving in a position of leadership. (5) They find it easy to make decisions. (6) They are willing and able to delegate authority.[51]

The need of the church for the exercise of the gift of leadership is quite obvious. As a general rule, anyone chairing a board or committee should possess this gift. Anyone serving as a congregational president, or elder/deacon board chairman, or planning committee chairman should possess this gift. The gift of leadership is necessary for giving direction and organization to God's people. While not every individual with pastoral responsibilities possesses the gift, it is an essential part of the gift mix in every pastoral team. This whole concept of gifts and gift mix is a strong argument for plurality of eldership within the local church.

Paul wrote that the gift of leadership should be exercised "with diligence," *en spoude* (Romans 12:8). *Spoude* suggests speed and dedication. The word can mean "to make haste; to be zealous, active, concerned about; to push on with something quickly; to be diligent; to be eager to serve; to be serious."[52] In Romans 12:8 it has the force of "with true commitment. What is meant is the holy zeal which demands full dedication to serving the community."[53] Paul's exhortation, then, is that the gift of leadership be exercised with full commitment to the needs and goals of the community and with maximum effort and speed.

The spiritually gifted leader works tirelessly to develop ways and means to achieve Spirit-directed goals. He will view the exercise of his gift as a means of helping his local body of believers to achieve the goals God has in mind.

SELF-EVALUATION

	Yes	No
1. Am I motivated to care for others?	❏	❏
2. Do I assume leadership when no leader is present?	❏	❏

	Yes	No
3. Am I able to organize and motivate people?	☐	☐
4. Do I find it easy to make decisions?	☐	☐
5. Do I have the ability to delegate?	☐	☐
6. As a result of my efforts are goals set?	☐	☐
7. As a result of my efforts are plans laid out to achieve the goals?	☐	☐
8. As a result of my efforts are people motivated to implement plans?	☐	☐
9. Are the projects I am involved in on the way to completion?	☐	☐

If most of your answers are yes, you may possess the gift of leadership.

MERCY

The term "mercy" occurs frequently in Old and New Testaments alike. In the Old Testament we read of the covenant mercy of God that causes Him to view us through the prejudiced eyes of a loving Father looking after His own children. The thought is carried over into the New Testament, where the Greek *eleos* is used instead of the Hebrew terms *cheseth* and *rhakum*.

Eleos means "pity, sympathy, loving-kindness."[54] It was the term used in Luke 10:37 to describe the deed of the good Samaritan. Mercy is an emotion that leads to action. This emotion is also described as "a feeling of sympathy, fellow-feeling with misery, compassion."[55] Perhaps the best translation of *eleos* is the literal meaning of our term "compassion." To have compassion is "to feel passion with" or "to commiserate." Mercy is more than sympathy or feeling sorry *for;* it is empathy or feeling sorry *with.* When we feel exactly what another feels, we understand better why he acts the way he does; this understanding meters our response. While grace gives people something that they do not deserve (unmerited favor), mercy withholds something that they do deserve (usually judgment).

What then is the spiritual gift of mercy? McQuay said, "It is the ability to demonstrate with joy heart-sympathy with the needs of others."[56] McRae wrote, "It is the capacity to perform deeds of mercy."[57] Ryrie commented, "It is akin to the gift of ministering... succoring those who are sick and afflicted."[58] John Packo said, "It is the Spirit-given ability to work compassionately and cheerfully with neglected people."[59] Peter Wagner wrote, "The gift of Mercy is the special ability that God gives to certain members of the Body of Christ to feel genuine empathy and compassion for individuals, both Christian and non-Christian...and to translate that compassion into cheerfully doing deeds that reflect Christ's love and alleviate the suffering."[60]

Paul admonished the one exercising the gift of mercy to do so "with cheerfulness" (Romans 12:8). The word translated "cheerfulness" is *hilarotes,* which means "cheerfulness, gladness, graciousness."[61] *Hilaros,* the adjective form of *hilarotes,* is translated "cheerful" in 2 Corinthians 9:7. Paul used *hilaros* there to show the opposite of "grudgingly or of necessity." The word translated "grudgingly" *(lupe)* refers to "pain or sorrow."[62] The phrase translated "not grudgingly" *(me ek lupes)* means "not reluctantly."[63] The phrase translated "not...of necessity" *(me ek anagkes)* means "not out of compulsion or necessity."[64] Thus *hilaros* must mean, at least in part, to be cheerfully willing and to be personally motivated by desire. So in Romans 12:8 Paul was urging those with the gift of mercy to exercise their gift only as they are motivated by the Holy Spirit of God. Otherwise they fail to exercise this spiritual gift as intended.

One of the best Scriptural examples of a person who showed mercy is the good Samaritan. While the parable encourages all believers to show mercy, perhaps there is a special lesson in the story for those who have the spiritual gift of mercy. The Samaritan's sole motivation for helping was compassion. He saw a man hurt and without hesitation did everything in his power to help. Once the Samaritan was finished, he left. What a tremendous ministry such a person has today! His soothing words are like balm on a wound. Then once the crisis has eased, he seems to melt into the woodwork until the need for his gift again motivates him to action.

The person possessing the gift of mercy will exercise it through a one-on-one relationship. He will seek out those who need help. He will be characterized by kindness and a very soft heart.[65] He will be extremely sensitive to the spiritual, emotional, and physical needs of others.[66] Thus his ministry will be with the bereaved, ill, anxious, depressed, poor, widow, and orphan.[67] He will find great joy and satisfaction in helping those with problems. He will be attracted to those in distress. You will find him working with shut-ins, doing hospital visitation, delivering food baskets to the poor, and ready to go at a moment's notice to those in need.[68]

Proof that a person possesses the gift of mercy can be given by those who have been the recipients of his ministry. They talk about the great comfort they have received, about the time that has been spent with them, and about the compassionate heart that has been shared. They all mention that when they needed him, he was there.

Deacon Bill Halliwell possesses the gift of mercy. There never was a man who cared more than Bill cares. Whenever there is a crisis or need in his congregation, Bill is there. He does not have to be called and asked to come; he automatically appears. When I was the pastor of his church and we went visiting together, I often sat and marveled as I saw his gift in operation. When one family in the church was in a near-fatal car crash, putting mother, father, and all six children in the hospital, Bill was the second person to reach the hospital. While the mother, Jean, was on the critical list, he would often appear late at night by her bedside because he felt a real compulsion from the Lord to be there. Bill would always arrive just when Jean needed him most. The doctors got the credit for healing Jean, but she insists to this day that Bill's loving compassion, concern, and care saw her through those critical hours and, by God's grace, gave her the desire to hang on. This story is only one of many that could be told about Bill's ministry. Now we live two hours away from Bill, but if I were to pick up the phone and call for help, in two hours Bill would be here—whether or not he was at work, whether or not he had other plans. What a comforting assurance this is.

Showing mercy is an especially vital ministry. What people need most is to be ministered to in times when they hurt, in times of bereavement and sorrow, in times of crisis and extreme anxiety.

SELF-EVALUATION

	Yes	No
1. Do I function best in one-on-one relationships?	❑	❑
2. Do I seek out those in need of help?	❑	❑
3. Do I have a soft heart?	❑	❑
4. Am I ready to go at a moment's notice?	❑	❑
5. Am I motivated by the hurt others feel?	❑	❑
6. Do others feel great relief and comfort when I visit them?	❑	❑
7. Do others feel the warmth of being loved and cared for when I am around?	❑	❑
8. Do I form intimate bonds with the people I try to help?	❑	❑

If most of your answers are yes, you may possess the gift of mercy.

Have you spotted yourself in any of these descriptions of people possessing serving gifts? Do any of these gifts seem to be yours? Put a mental check mark beside the ones that do. Also make a mental note of the gifts that definitely are not yours. This self-evaluation may help narrow the field as you try to pinpoint your spiritual gifts a bit later.

6

INTERACTIONS

Having considered all of the spiritual gifts that are for today, we can now build a scenario and show how each gift would naturally respond to a given situation. Here is the situation: A member of a local church fell off a ladder while he was painting his garage. He broke a leg and he is now lying in the hospital with his leg in traction. A variety of people from his church come to visit. Each visitor possesses a different spiritual gift and responds differently to the situation. Let's call our hapless victim "Bill" and ask ourselves, "Which of Bill's visitors is most like me?"

PROPHET. Hi, Bill. You know, we often do not know why God allows these things to happen, but we know God has a purpose. Sometimes He is trying to get our attention, to put His finger on some area of our lives. What about you, Bill? Can you think of anything the Lord might possibly be trying to say to you? [If you have a church full of prophets, pray they do not all come in the same evening!]

TEACHER. Hi, Bill. Sorry to hear about your accident. I have been doing some studying for a series in Sunday school on suffering. Let me share just a few of the marvelous truths God has for us in His Word on this subject. I will leave this fourteen-page outline with you so that you can study further at your own leisure.

PASTOR/TEACHER. Hi, Bill. I got here as soon as I heard. What happened? What is the prognosis? How long will you be laid up? Just want you to know that we love you and miss you. Is there anything we can do for you? Let me share some Scripture with you [usually of comfort and assurance rather than didactic in nature] and then we will pray together.

71

GIVER. Hi, Bill. Just dropped in to see how you are feeling. I stopped at the desk and the receptionist said you did not have TV. It's going to be turned on—"compliments of the house." Bill, I know how expensive hospital stays can be and how insurance often does not cover everything, but don't worry. I am sure that the Lord will supply your need. By the way, the cashier told me that although Blue Cross only pays a portion, the total cost of your room is already covered for the next two weeks. Isn't that fantastic?

EXHORTER. Hi, Bill. How are you feeling? It's not too difficult to see how this accident happened. (a) You tried to do the job alone. (b) Your ladder had no cleats on the legs. (c) Standing your ladder on top of that fifty-five-gallon drum to get more height wasn't very smart! Next time call me. I have an extension ladder with cleats. You hold the ladder, and I'll climb. We'll get that garage done. Deal?

ADMINISTRATOR. Hi, Bill. Just stopped by to see how you are doing. Now don't worry about a thing while you are here. We've organized transportation to take your children to school; my wife is lending her car to your wife; and we've planned a painting party at your house on Saturday to finish the garage. By the way, Bill, what were you doing with that fifty-five-gallon drum?

SERVER. Hi, Bill. How are you feeling today? Here's a crossword-puzzle book you might like. Had a chance to take your son with me to his Little League game last night. His team won 6-3 and he got two hits. Also got your grass mowed today—had to do mine anyway—and I noticed some holes and bare spots. I took the liberty of filling them in and spreading some seed; hope you don't mind. I'll be in later on Saturday because a bunch of us are going to do some painting. By the way, I cleaned all the spilled paint off your driveway, but I couldn't get it all off that fifty-five-gallon drum.

MERCY. Hi, Bill. I came up as soon as I heard. Tell me how it happened. Here, let me prop up your pillow a bit. Want some water? Can I get you anything? I sat with your wife while you were in the emergency room and through your surgery, and she's holding up well. I know it's 10:00 p.m., but I just wanted to stop in and pray with you. I know you are hurting so I won't stay long. Let's just pray together and I'll stop by in the morning on my way to work.

By the time all the visitors have come, Bill is on cloud nine. He has been totally ministered to by the body of Christ. Each visitor, through the exercise of his/her gift, has responded to his need. He will sleep well tonight, knowing he is surrounded by a loving, caring, sharing family of believers. He is well-assured that his wife and family will be cared for while he is laid up and that the normal household chores will be taken care of. This scenario pictures the body of Christ at work—functioning the way it is intended to function.

For the body to function smoothly, the parts need to work together without friction. To avoid friction, the members need to understand the gifts of others. We need to recognize the validity and the particular emphases of those who have gifts we do not possess. Their particular gift-mix will color the way they view certain situations, the conclusions they draw, and the way they react. We need to consider differences in the gifts so we can better understand other believers. As we make some comparisons, analyze your own emphases and reactions. This analysis may help you identify your own gifts.

EMPHASES

The speaking gifts, for example, are all motivational in character, but their emphases vary. (See comparison on page 51.) When the gift of evangelism, for instance, is exercised, the hearer will become keenly aware of his need of Christ and His redemption and will cry out in repentance and faith. When the gift of prophecy is exercised, the believer will become very aware of sin in his life and will cry out to the Lord for forgiveness and restoration. The difference is the audience. The message of evangelism is directed to the lost; the message of the prophet is directed to the Lord's people.

If we compare the prophet and the teacher, we see a difference in focus. The teacher begins with a desire to expound the Word; the prophet begins with a desire to expose sin and produce holiness in the lives of believers. Unlike the teacher, the prophet's expertise is not in deep exposition or systematic study of the Scriptures.

Since Paul listed teaching and exhortation separately in Romans 12:7-8, he must have intended a distinction between these two gifts as well. McRae said that the gift of exhortation "enables the believer to effectively urge someone to pursue a course of conduct. If the response to the teacher is 'I see that!', then the response to the exhorter would be 'I will do that!'"[1] John Walvoord said, "Exhortation is presenting truth in such a way as to stir to action. The exhorter is not necessarily a good Bible teacher."[2] Walvoord also stated, "Exhortation is an appeal to action, and is the practical application of the teaching ministry."[3] Exhortation is a "summons to the will, an appeal—urgent, persuasive, and authoritative."[4] The exercise of the gift of teaching appeals to the intellect; the exercise of the gift of exhortation appeals to the will. The teacher will study, organize, and then present; the exhorter will exhort and then find Scripture to back up the exhortation.

There are differences among the serving gifts as well. For example, unlike the helper who does any job that needs to be done, the leader will organize and delegate the task, probably to a helper. The leader takes the vision of the dreamer (the one who has the gift of faith) and lays out a plan of attack to make the vision a reality.

REACTIONS

With the varying emphases come varying reactions to situations. Conflicts may arise when we do not understand each other's reactions.

For example, the prophet may experience conflicts with other members of the body. Prophecy is not the gift to possess if one's goal is popularity. Yet the prophet who lacks understanding may be intolerant of those who do not see truth as clearly as he does. He may think a teacher is compromising and not teaching the truth because he is not involved in an iconoclastic ministry. In a counseling situation a prophet may exhibit intolerance of a counselee who does not heed his counsel and do what he says.

A church member with the gift of evangelism may come into conflict with a member possessing the gift of shepherding or the gift of teaching. The main thrust of the shepherd or teacher will be the edification of the body of Christ, and the evangelist who does not understand other gifts may be upset on the Sundays when the sermon lacks an evangelistic emphasis. The evangelist may want altar calls every week, while the pastor/teacher may feel that certain messages do not logically lead to altar calls for salvation. The evangelist may become "transient" if the particular church he is a part of does not share his zeal for the lost and provide opportunities for him and others to use the gift of evangelism.

The evangelist needs to realize that the bulk of evangelism takes place outside the church and that the primary task of the shepherd is to equip the saints. The shepherd, on the other hand, needs to realize the possibility of there being unsaved people in every service. He should attempt to make the claims of Christ clear in each message and be sensitive to the leading of the Holy Spirit regarding altar calls. Both the evangelist and the shepherd are needed. The lost must be reached; new converts must be discipled. A healthy, thriving church needs both gifts to operate together harmoniously.

Believers with the gift of faith have altered the course of history and have been the agents through whom the church has made great leaps forward. But many with this gift have been stifled by the shortsightedness of others. Such a person will have difficulty understanding the plodding "system" and its lack of vision. He will often become irritated by criticism; he will tend to be impatient with those who do not "see" his vision.[5] If the person who possesses the gift of faith does not have a tolerant attitude toward the gifts and subsequent viewpoints of others,

he will become frustrated very quickly with the average con-
servative church board. The universal church of Christ and local churches individually need to be sensitive to the exercise of
this gift in their midst.

The person with the gift of leadership may be confronted with
opposition if he does not exercise his gift in love (see 1
Corinthians 13). He may exhibit a tendency to drive people instead of leading them. If he is not sensitive to the gifts of others
who do not share his emphasis, he may be irritated if his plan of
attack is not immediately grasped by others or if his committee
does not progress quickly in the execution of his plan.

CONCLUSION

Barnabas, who has been mentioned before, is a good example
of someone who exercised his own gifts, recognized which gifts
were not his, and understood the gifts of others. In the book of
Acts he is always shown quietly ministering to others. He was
prompted by human need. He possessed an ability to size up a
situation, draw a conclusion, and then take action on the basis
of the conclusion.

Our first glimpse of Barnabas is in Acts 4:34-37. His heart
was aching for his brothers and sisters in Christ who were in
great need because of persecution. He sold his holdings and
quietly gave the proceeds to the apostles to distribute as needed.

We see the next cameo in Acts 9:23-31. Saul of Tarsus said
he had been converted, but none of the disciples believed him.
They thought the story was only a ruse to help Saul find out
who all the believers were. The body of believers locked him
out of their fellowship. Rejected by Christians and hunted by
the religious leaders of Jewry, Saul faced a future that did not
look rosy. Then Barnabas entered the picture. He had the God-
given ability to read the situation and assess the validity of Saul's
testimony. Saul and Barnabas began a friendship that would last
a long while.

We see Barnabas again in Acts 11:22-26. The church at
Jerusalem recognized Barnabas's gifts and sent him as their
emissary to find out what was happening in Antioch, where many

were being converted. Once Barnabas arrived in Antioch, he exhorted the Christians there, but he realized they had a need he could not fill. They needed a teacher. Immediately he headed for Tarsus to find the man with the spiritual gifts to fill the need: Paul (Saul). Barnabas and Paul copastored the church at Antioch for a whole year and the church experienced great blessing and growth. What a winning combination! Paul—the great expounder of the Word of God; the man with the great prophetic gift; the man who saw only black and white, no shades; the bombastic proclaimer of "thus saith the Lord"—was coupled with Barnabas, the great one-on-one worker. Barnabas was gentler than Paul and perhaps more sensitive to the feelings of others.

In Acts 11:29-30 we see Barnabas and Paul being sent back to the church at Jerusalem with gifts from the church at Antioch. Barnabas must have told the Christians in Antioch of his heartache for the suffering brethren in Jerusalem.

We see Barnabas and Paul again in Acts 13–14 as the first missionary team sent out by the church to reach the lost.

Our last glimpse of Barnabas is in Acts 15:36-41. At first glance this picture looks negative, but it may well be the most telling of all. There was a sharp division between Barnabas and Paul over whether or not to take John Mark on the second missionary journey. He had gone with them on the first trip, only to get "cold feet" in Turkey and go home. Barnabas wanted to give John Mark a second chance, but Paul was emphatic in his refusal. Paul and Barnabas split company. Paul took Silas and revisited the churches, while Barnabas and Mark headed to Cyprus to plow new ground. Barnabas is not mentioned again, while Paul's life fills the rest of Acts.

Does Scripture thus vindicate Paul and vilify Barnabas? Many a preacher has given this impression. But before you accept this interpretation, think about Paul's last words to Timothy (2 Timothy 4:11): "Get Mark and bring him with you [to see me], for he is useful to me for ministry." A lot of water and years had passed over the dam since that first missionary trip and John Mark had fully redeemed himself in the mind of Paul. But Barnabas had seen potential in John Mark from the beginning. Barnabas had known immediately what took Paul the rest of his life to conclude. Much like Saul, who might never have been accepted by the believers in Jerusalem if Barnabas had not befriended him, John Mark might have borne the scars of failure forever and never written the second Gospel if Barnabas had not encouraged him.

The life of Barnabas illustrates two principles that we need to apply to our lives. First, Barnabas knew that he was gifted. He was confident in his gifts and he used them. For example, wherever there were personal problems, he exercised his gift of exhortation. He knew what caused each problem and how to solve it. He was a great trouble-shooter and also a great counselor. You and I also have gifts. We must use them because they are needed by the body of Christ.

Second, Barnabas knew his limitations. He knew that there were other believers who could do certain jobs much better than he could. Barnabas knew that he and Paul had different spiritual gifts and different contributions to make to the body of Christ. He respected Paul's approach to problems even though his approach was different. Similarly, you and I have varying mindsets and solutions, depending on which gifts we possess, and we need to be able to see each other's slants on a problem. My gift is part of the solution and your gift is part of the solution. Together we can solve the problem and the body of Christ will be the beneficiary.

7

HOW CAN I IDENTIFY
MY SPIRITUAL GIFTS?

A ll of the preceding material was only a long hallway to chan-
nel us into this room where each of us can deal with the question, How can I identify my spiritual gifts? Before coming to
grips with the question, we need to review the conclusions we
drew from Ephesians 4:16 and 1 Corinthians 12:7,11: (1) God's
pattern for a growing, healthy church involves the participation
of each member of the body for the mutual good; (2) every member is specially equipped by the Holy Spirit of God with spiritual
gifts; (3) the members of the body minister to one another and
build up the body through the exercise of their spiritual gifts.
These verses remind us of the importance of finding our spiritual
gifts.[1]

As we try to pinpoint our gifts, we need to remember that the
Holy Spirit sovereignly dispenses His gifts. The gift list is not a
department store where we go to shop. The list is a measurement
tool we use to see where we fit. As Peter Wagner said: "It is not
up to you, as a Christian, to place an order for the gifts which you
might want. God, by His grace...gives us the gifts....Then, our
first responsibility is to discover our gifts."[2]

We can find our spiritual gifts by following the steps in a four-
fold progression: comprehension, evaluation, experimentation,
and confirmation. If we follow these steps in this order, we will
narrow down and with some degree of accuracy pinpoint our gifts.

COMPREHENSION

The first step in finding our spiritual gifts is understanding
the facts: what spiritual gifts are, when and how we get them,

how they are to be used, and what their characteristics are. The previous chapters of this handbook were intended to provide comprehension on a Biblical basis. There are some other excellent books on the subject (Peter Wagner, Donald MacGavran, John Packo, Earl McQuay, and Leslie Flynn are a few of the authors I recommend) and the more we read about gifts, the better our comprehension will be.

EVALUATION

The process of evaluation has also probably already begun. Hopefully as you read the previous chapters, noted the characteristics of people possessing each of the gifts, and completed the self-evaluations, your mind crossed some gifts off the list, put question marks by others, and put check marks by still others. When you mentally crossed off one gift, you may have said, "That is definitely not my gift!" When you checked another, you may have had the "Nathanael experience": How did you know me? (John 1:45-51) This is all part of what I call *informal* evaluation. Informal evaluation also involves analyzing your desires[3]—thinking about what you enjoy doing or would like to try to do. To crystallize the informal evaluation, fill in the following chart. Check one column for each gift.

INFORMAL EVALUATION CHART

Do I possess the gift of...	Yes	Probably	Possibly	No
Prophecy?				
Evangelism?				
Shepherding?				
Teaching?				
Exhortation?				
Faith?				
Helps/Ministering (Serving)?				
Giving?				
Administration/Leadership?				
Mercy?				

A *formal* evaluation is accomplished through the use of a testing device. There are literally scores of testing vehicles for determining one's spiritual gifts.[4] For the money there is no better test than the one put out by the Christian Reformed Church Home Missions. I have adapted their questionnaire to suit the purposes of this handbook and have included the revised version in appendix C.[5] No test is absolutely foolproof, but this simple questionnaire could be a great aid in helping you discover your gifts. You should turn to appendix C and take this formal test before you read on.

After completing your informal and formal evaluations and comparing the results on pages 80 and 104, group the gifts under three headings in the following table.

I Gifts I am sure I possess	II Gifts I am sure I do not possess	III Gifts that do not belong in columns I and II
_____	_____	_____
_____	_____	_____
_____	_____	_____
_____	_____	_____
_____	_____	_____

EXPERIMENTATION

Through informal and formal evaluations the list has been narrowed down and you are ready to take the next step. (Many books on spiritual gifts end with discovery, but this handbook goes further.) In this phase of the progression, each gift you listed in column I in the above table should be run, one by one, through the process of experimentation.

The experimentation phase could also be called the apprenticeship phase. When you reach this phase, you serve a four-week apprenticeship in an area or areas where a particular gift would function. Your performance during this period will provide a sense of whether or not you possess the gift. You should serve one apprenticeship for each of the gifts listed in column I on page 81.

You, as the apprentice, should be paired with someone who can make an evaluation of your performance. We will refer to this person as your trainer or mentor. Your trainer needs to have an understanding of spiritual gifts as a whole and an understanding of what to look for when he assesses your performance.

Your church should set up apprenticeships for the process of experimentation. For several of the gifts, the apprenticeship vehicle is already in place. For instance, a Sunday school class can provide an opportunity to test for the gift of teaching. For other gifts, the church will have to use some ingenuity to create the vehicle. Appendix D offers ideas of areas where the possession of each gift can be assessed.

For this apprenticeship or experimentation phase to be effective, there must be a control and an evaluation tool. A control is a non-moving anchor against which achievement can be measured. In this case the control consists of (1) the curriculum and (2) the trainer or mentor.

The curriculum should expose the apprentice to as much experimentation as possible. The more opportunities he has to exercise a gift, the better the final assessment will be. The curriculum will vary depending on the apprenticeship vehicle; for instance, a person can easily make visits on three different days during a week, but he would find it difficult to teach three different times during a week.

The trainer or mentor will be the major evaluator. In many cases the mentor is already there—Sunday school teacher, youth sponsor, pastor, or elder. In other cases a mentor needs to be found.

An evaluation tool is included in appendix E. This tool is simple and deals with concretes that can be measured. It is based on the characteristics of individuals possessing each gift and the results of the exercise of the gift. Make copies of the appropriate pages so that you and your trainer can fill out separate sheets at the end of each opportunity to exercise a gift. At the end of each apprenticeship period, you and your trainer should discuss all the evaluations and come to a conclusion about whether or not you possess the spiritual gift.

By the time you have completed the informal and formal evaluations, served an apprenticeship for each gift you think you possess, and discussed your findings with your mentor, you should know what your spiritual gifts are.

CONFIRMATION

Once you have identified your gifts, select one at a time and find a niche to use it. Over a two-month period look at the product or results of the exercise of that gift. Confirmation is based on your own evaluation of these results, the evaluation of those you serve, and the evaluation of a mentor.

For instance, if your gift is teaching, then teach. During the two-month confirmation process evaluate your own work. Do you find it exciting to teach the Word of God to others? Do you find it easy to study, present lessons, and field questions? Does the light go on in your students' eyes while you are teaching them? Do your students learn? Next consider your students' evaluation. Do they feel that they are learning what you are teaching? Finally take into account your mentor's evaluation of the results.

If the three evaluations are positive, your possession of the gift has been confirmed. Further confirmation will be provided by the unique joy or exuberance that fills your heart each time you use your gift.

Pastor John White tells an interesting story concerning the discovery of his spiritual gift. First Dr. White discovered what it was not. Since his first choice for validation was the gift of evangelism, he borrowed some excellent proven-effective messages from some great evangelists. He delivered the sermons with some of the mannerisms of Jack Wyrtzen, and loudly and enthusiastically proclaimed the Word. But the audience were glued to their seats, so he concluded that his gift was not evangelism. A while later he was asked to teach a men's Bible class—a large class of older men who had been saved before he was born. He felt inadequate but decided to teach the book of Ephesians verse-by-verse from the Greek. During class he noticed several men wiping away tears and afterward some of the students pointed out marvelous truths the Holy Spirit had revealed to them through his teaching. Dr. White discovered that at least one of his gifts was teaching.

If you have followed the steps of comprehension, evaluation, experimentation, and confirmation, you probably have experienced the same satisfaction that Dr. White felt when he discovered his spiritual gift.

CONCLUSION

Now you know what part of the body you are and how God has specially gifted you to function. Paul exhorted Timothy to "stir up [literally, rekindle the fire] the gift of God which is in you" (2 Timothy 1:6) and I would pass this exhortation on to you. You know what your gifts are, so look for opportunities to use them. Remember, having one particular gift does not lock you into only one type of ministry. There are a variety of ways each gift can be expressed and a variety of avenues through which each gift can be exercised. Look for tasks that your gifts can accomplish.

You only have a certain amount of time for service, so do not spend time trying to do a task for which you are not equipped. God has someone else equipped for that particular task. Get yourself plugged into the local body of Christ and enjoy the satisfaction and blessing that come from working within the sphere of your own spiritual gifts. Once your church leaders become aware of your spiritual gifts, they will probably seek you out and encourage you to use your gifts for the good of the body. If they do not, volunteer your services in those areas where you are gifted. When you serve within the appropriate sphere, your productivity will increase and you will experience the great joy that comes from being used by God to bless the lives of others.

Remember, Ephesians 4:16 states God's program for church growth. So go get busy!

—THE BEGINNING—

Appendix A
Sign/Revelatory Gifts

Sign gifts include healings, miracles, tongues, and interpretation of tongues. These gifts were given to God's prophets and apostles in the first century A.D. to validate them as messengers sent from God. Since the New Testament was still in the process of being written, anyone could claim that he had received a message from God. People needed signs to help them distinguish true messengers from false ones.

In Acts 2:22 Peter referred to Christ as "Jesus of Nazareth, a Man attested by God to you by miracles, wonders, and signs which God did through Him." The word translated "attested" means "to proclaim, show forth, display, exhibit."[1] God fully proved and clearly demonstrated that Jesus was the Messiah and His Son. The means He used to attest these facts were miracles, wonders, and signs.

Hebrews 2:3-4 shows that God used the same method to validate the original apostles who were eyewitnesses of Christ's life and work: "God also bearing witness both with signs and wonders, with various miracles, and gifts of the Holy Spirit, according to His own will." Paul too made it quite clear that there was a definite group of signs that identified one as a true messenger of God: "Truly the signs of an apostle were accomplished among you with all perseverance, in signs and wonders and mighty deeds" (2 Corinthians 12:12).

Once the need for giving authentication ceased, so did the Biblical exercise of the accompanying sign gifts.

Revelatory gifts include apostle, prophet, word of wisdom, word of knowledge, and discernment of spirits. God used these gifts in the giving of revelation. The apostles were the proclaimers of the truth presented by Christ (Hebrews 2:3-4). They were with Jesus from His baptism to His resurrection and were part of the foundational blocks of the church. Their work was finished when the apostle John died and the office ceased with his death.

The prophet—in the primary sense—was a receiver and proclaimer of direct revelation from God. This office ceased with the completion of the Canon. Once revelation was written there was no more new communication coming from God, so prophecy as a revelatory gift was no longer needed by A.D. 100.[2]

Two other revelatory gifts, mentioned together by Paul, are word of knowledge and word of wisdom.[3] The term translated "word" is *logos,* which indicates a word, a piece, a part—a small fragment as opposed to the whole. The emphasis of *logos* would be on not having all knowledge or all wisdom, but a part or a piece of it. Both "word of knowledge" and "word of wisdom" are hopoxlegomenas, 1 Corinthians 12:8 being the only place in Scripture where the phrases are used. The terms "knowledge" and "wisdom" are prevalent, but not in this particular format.

Riggs defined "word of knowledge" as "God's knowledge…it is revelation of facts and happenings."[4] Carlson defined the gift as "divine communication by revelation of facts relating to earth which are not known."[5] John Calvin said it is "supernatural revelation by the Holy Spirit, facts in the mind of God, a divinely given fragment of divine knowledge, and not a God-sent amplification of human knowledge."[6] Jepson said it is "a supernatural impartation of fact in the mind of God to the mind of the believer. It is not all but a fragment. It is an item of information the believer could not learn by observation/investigation."[7] The common denominator of these definitions is the revelational character of the word of knowledge. God used this gift to provide man with information that he could receive in no other way.

This gift was extremely valuable to the early church, especially to teachers in the first century. Baxter said the word of knowledge "was a special gift that enabled the first century believer to know and instruct the assembly in the truth of the continuing New Testament. It went far beyond normal and natural capacities of knowledge."[8] McRae said the gift "was the ability to understand correctly and exhibit clearly the spiritual wisdom God revealed to and by the apostles….It was a temporary gift [noting 1 Corinthians 13:8], foundational in character, and particularly needful for the teacher in the infant Church as the New Testament had not yet been completed."[9]

The word of wisdom is also revelational in character. McRae said, "It is the capacity to receive revealed truth from God and present it to the people of God."[10] Baxter said, "It is the immediate grasp of the secret plans and purposes of God....This information became Scripture."[11] Charles Hodge said that the word of wisdom "was a characteristic gift of the apostles and prophets, involved in the process of receiving direct revelation from God, and existed in the first century before the completion of the Canon."[12] This gift was associated with the transmission of revelation and the protection of the truth while the Canon was being completed.

Once the foundation of the apostles and prophets had been laid and the completed Canon had become the yardstick for measuring and determining truth, the word of knowledge and the word of wisdom (component parts of the process of revelation) became obsolete.

The gift of discernment too is revelational in nature. The word used to designate this gift is *diakrisis,* from the verb *diakrino,* meaning "to evaluate, judge, recognize, discern, make a distinction."[13] *Diakrino* has the connotation of "to make a distinction, differentiate, judge correctly, pass judgment, render a decision."[14] There is little doubt that the gift of discernment was used to discern between that which is false and that which is true.[15]

When we study the New Testament passages cited as examples of the use of the gift of discernment (Acts 13:8-11, for instance) we find that it was expressed by those who possessed other foundational gifts. First Corinthians 14:32 says, "The spirits of the prophets are subject to the prophets." This verse gives the test for orthodoxy during the period when the New Testament was still in the process of being transmitted. Any prophetic message had to be validated by a consensus of those in the church who were prophets, those who had been used to communicate revelation to the church. The exercise of the spiritual gift of discernment was part of the process used by this "guardian board" to determine what was truth. As Lambert wrote,

"With prophecy must be associated discernment of spirits—the first is a gift for the speaker...the second, a gift for the receiver."[16]

Ryrie said the gift of discernment was the "ability to distinguish true and false sources of supernatural revelation given in oral form."[17] Walvoord wrote, "It was a fail-safe detection device especially desperately needed by the early church. Once the New Testament was completed, the written word performed this work; this gift was no longer necessary."[18] Baxter noted, "We need discernment today... but [that discernment] is based upon the Word of God."[19] As Sanders said, "So long as there was no written New Testament, it was a gift of special importance."[20] McRae concluded: "It was the capacity to determine if a teacher, prophet, preacher was speaking by the Holy Spirit, his own human spirit, or an evil spirit. It was extremely important to the early Church, because it had no New Testament as yet for the standard. It was a temporary, foundational gift, whose need was eliminated by the completed Canon."[21]

Today we have a standard by which we can measure the validity of any message or messenger: God's completed Word. All we need to do is apply God's ruler and see if what is said measures up. First John 4:1 urges all believers not to believe every spirit, but to "test the spirits, whether they are of God." The word translated "test" here is *dokimazo,* which means to "put to the test, examine, try to learn, prove by testing."[22] This process of testing the spirits is different from the application of the spiritual gift of discernment, which enables one to sift truth and error immediately. Although the gift of discernment is not for today, we certainly still have the responsibility to test the spirits.

Each of the sign/revelatory gifts was temporary in nature, like the space shuttle's solid rocket boosters, which are unnecessary and nonfunctional after liftoff and insertion speed are achieved. These gifts were needed to establish the foundation of the church and to provide it with God's last volume of divine revelation: the New Testament. Once these two ends were achieved, these gifts ceased to function.

APPENDIX B
OTHER CANDIDATES

Nineteen spiritual gifts are included in the Scriptural list cited in chapter 3. However, some authors suggest other candidates for the title of spiritual gift. We will consider a few of them in this appendix.

HOSPITALITY

The term translated "hospitality" is a compound word, *philoxenos,* formed from *phileo* meaning "to love or to have brotherly love for" and *zenos* meaning "stranger." Thus a hospitable person is a stranger-lover. Hospitality was an earmark of the early church. "One of the most prominent features in the pictures of early Christianity, which is so rich in good works, is undoubtedly its hospitality. Witness is borne to this by both friend and foe alike."[1] I do not question the validity of the concept of hospitality as a duty of the body of Christ, but I do question its designation as a spiritual gift.

John Packo defined hospitality as "the ability to cheerfully make guests, known or unknown, feel at home within our household."[2] He called hospitality a gift on the basis of 1 Peter 4:9-10. Hospitality can also be defined as "the ability to welcome and graciously serve guests or strangers" (Romans 12:13).[3] Peter Wagner used almost the same terminology: "the special ability God gives to certain members of the Body of Christ to provide an open house and warm welcome for those in need of food and lodging."[4]

Whose designation is the most Biblical? Does the same reasoning that applies to the gift of giving apply to hospitality? All believers are urged to give (1 Corinthians 16:1-4; 2 Corinthians

8–9). Giving is part of our worship. But beyond the duty and responsibility of every believer to give is the spiritual gift of giving. Likewise all believers are told to exhort one another and provoke one another to good works (Hebrews 10:24-25). But beyond this responsibility is the spiritual gift of exhortation. Hospitality too is the duty of all Christians, but is there a sense in which hospitality is a spiritual gift? Let us look for the answer in Scripture.

Romans 12:13

In the midst of many exhortations, Romans 12:13 states that a believer should be "given to hospitality." The word translated "given" means "zealously follow, to run after, to attach oneself to, or to earnestly pursue or promote."[5] Paul used the same word in Romans 14:19 where he said, "Pursue the things which make for peace." In the same way that the believers in Rome were to set a course, run after, and pursue the things that make for peace, they were to follow after and practice hospitality. An expanded translation of Romans 12:13 might read, "Continually be practicing and looking for opportunities to express hospitality." Romans 12:13 is a general exhortation given to all believers in Rome and, by application, to us as well.

Many people might like to define hospitality as a spiritual gift (which they do not possess) because they would thus be excused from the responsibility to be hospitable. But even if hospitality is found to be a spiritual gift in a different context, Romans 12:13 lays the responsibility at the feet of every believer in Christ. Here Paul was not talking about hospitality as a spiritual gift, but he was definitely speaking of our responsibility. He not only told us to be hospitable; he told us to look for opportunities to fulfill this obligation!

1 Peter 4:9

The context of 1 Peter 4:9 is not much different from the context of Romans 12:13. In light of the approaching end of all things,

Peter gave five exhortations to be followed by all believers (4:7-11): be serious; be watchful in prayer; express fervent love among yourselves; be hospitable; and serve within the framework of your spiritual gifts.

First Peter 4:9 uses the plural noun from *philoxenos* with the verb "to be" understood; literally the verse reads, "Be hospitable to one another without grudging." The statement is a command, but to direct hospitality toward others in the body of Christ simply out of necessity or duty does not fulfill the obligation. (The word literally translated "grudging," *gongusmos,* means "complaint or displeasure expressed in murmuring; secret talk, whispering."[6]) "Sitting down on the outside and standing up on the inside" is not God's definition of obedience. Besides, how can a person be expressing true hospitality, which literally is brotherly love to strangers, when he is griping, muttering, and complaining?

Once again, the exhortation from Peter was directed to his entire audience as a command. The language he used suggests that hospitality is something about which there is no question; he expected hospitality to be a logical outcome of being a child of God.

1 Timothy 3:2; Titus 1:8

Nowhere in the contexts of these two verses do we find any mention of spiritual gifts. First Timothy 3:2 and Titus 1:8 use the noun *philoxenos* (the same form Peter used) to include hospitality in the list of the qualifications of a bishop/elder. An elder is not qualified by the possession of certain gifts, but by maturity and growth. Every newborn Christian is gifted by the Holy Spirit of God, but he certainly has not attained any measure of maturity. These two passages, then, say to me that hospitality is a byproduct of growth and therefore a litmus test for maturity. Every elder must be known as a man with an open home and an open heart. If a man does not possess this open-door attitude, he does not qualify as a candidate for the office of elder.

Every believer in Christ is urged and expected to have a hospitable attitude, and hospitality is one of the qualifications for eldership. But Scripture does not go beyond these injunctions. There is no mention of a special spiritual gift of hospitality in the Bible. However I do think that through hospitality the gifts of serving and giving can be expressed. For example, Martha (sister of Lazarus and Mary) expressed her gift of serving in an open home, an open hearth, and a table that always had room for more plates.

The conclusion I draw from Scripture is that hospitality is not a separate spiritual gift, but an avenue through which gifts of serving and giving can be expressed.

INTERCESSION

Peter Wagner gave no Scriptural basis for his belief that intercession is a spiritual gift but stated, "I have postulated the existence of this gift because I believe I have seen it in action."[7] My more narrow definition of spiritual gifts restricts the use of the term to those gifts that are listed in Scripture.

Certain believers have had extraordinary prayer ministries. The names and lives of "Praying Hyde" and George Muller come immediately to mind. But might not their intercession have been just an avenue through which their spiritual gift of faith was exercised? There is an inseparable link in Scripture between faith and prayer. In fact without faith, prayer is empty and doomed to nonproduction. James coupled faith and prayer when he said, "Let him ask in faith, with no doubting....The prayer of faith will save the sick" (James 1:6; 5:15). I see intercession as just one of the many channels through which the gift of faith can be exercised, and not as a separate spiritual gift.

POVERTY AND MARTYRDOM

According to Peter Wagner there are two more spiritual gifts in 1 Corinthians 13:3: voluntary poverty ("though I bestow all my goods to feed the poor")[8] and martyrdom ("though I give my body to be burned").[9] The verse does not label either poverty or martyrdom as a gift, and the syntax does not suggest the expectancy of reality. The attitude expressed in voluntary poverty could be a characteristic of someone possessing the spiritual gift of giving. If martyrdom were a spiritual gift, it could only be used once per person. These two suggestions do not fit my definition of spiritual gifts.

CELIBACY

Packo defined celibacy as "the ability to remain single without frustration."[10] The contention that celibacy is a spiritual gift does have a Scriptural base in 1 Corinthians 7:7. There Paul was talking about his unmarried state when he said, "For I wish that all men were even as I myself. But each one has his own gift *[charisma]* from God." We need to remember, however, that *charisma* is not used exclusively for spiritual gifts. All spiritual gifts are *charismata* (plural form of *charisma*), but the word is used as well to refer to salvation (Romans 6:23) and God's hand of protection (2 Corinthians 1:11). As a noun *charisma* means "gift" or "grace-gift" with the emphasis on the gracious nature of this act of giving. What we need to determine is whether the use of *charisma* in 1 Corinthians 7:7 automatically classifies celibacy as a spiritual gift, or Paul's use of the word is a generic reference to celibacy as a special grace given by God.

The unmarried state is not the norm, nor is it a requirement for Christian service. Peter had a mother-in-law who was healed, so he definitely was married. Paul's qualifications for elders in Timothy and Titus include being a good husband and father. Paul was only saying in 1 Corinthians 7:7 that because of the persecution of believers, it would be easier to be unmarried and to be exempt from the extra burden of worrying about family. His words were expedient for the specific time in which he wrote and were not meant to set a standard for the church.

My contention is that in 1 Corinthians 7:7 Paul used *charisma* in the generic sense to show that it takes a special measure of God's grace, a gift of grace, to remain unmarried. Celibacy is a

state totally opposed to all of the biological, social, and emotional needs built into man or woman by God. Only God was
able to overrule Paul's instincts and by grace control them so
that he could remain unmarried.

APPENDIX C
FORMAL TEST

INSTRUCTIONS

First: Rate yourself by completing the Gifts Analysis Questionnaire beginning on page 98.

Second: Compile the results by filling in the Key Chart on page 103.

GIFTS ANALYSIS QUESTIONNAIRE

The Following Is True of Me...

		(1) Very Little	(2) Little	(3) Some	(4) Much	(5) Very Much
1.	I am able to organize ideas, tasks, people, and time for Christian service.	☐	☐	☐	☑	☐
2.	I have been used to encourage people to live Christlike lives.	☐	☐	☑	☐	☐
3.	I like to talk about Jesus to those who don't know Him.	☐	☐	☑	☐	☐
4.	I have had the experience of knowing God's will with certainty in a specific situation even when concrete evidence was missing.	☐	☑	☐	☐	☐
5.	I assume responsibility for meeting financial needs in church and community.	☐	☐	☑	☐	☐
6.	I motivate groups toward specific Biblical objectives.	☐	☐	☑	☐	☐
7.	I have a knack for turning compassion into cheerful deeds of kindness.	☐	☐	☑	☐	☐
8.	I have pleaded the cause of God to the people of the church and/or world.	☐	☐	☑	☐	☐
9.	I enjoy doing tasks that help others minister effectively.	☐	☐	☐	☑	☐
10.	I have been responsible for the spiritual lives of Christians with good results.	☐	☐	☑	☐	☐
11.	Content "comes alive" for students (children or adults) when I teach.	☐	☐	☑	☐	☐
12.	I am sensitive to suffering, troubled, and discouraged people and want to help them see God's answers to life's problems.	☐	☐	☐	☑	☐

The Following Is True of Me...

	(1) Very Little	(2) Little	(3) Some	(4) Much	(5) Very Much
13. I would like to be able to share the gospel freely and effectively with unbelieving persons.	☐	☐	☐	☑	☐
14. I find myself accepting God's promises at face value and applying them to given situations without doubt.	☐	☐	☐	☑	☐
15. I feel moved to give when confronted with financial needs in God's kingdom.	☐	☐	☑	☐	☐
16. I would like to minister to those who have physical or mental problems.	☐	☐	☐	☑	☐
17. I have spiritual insights from the Scriptures relating to people and issues that make me want to speak out.	☐	☑	☐	☐	☐
18. I sense when others need a helping hand and am ready to give it.	☐	☐	☐	☑	☐
19. I am concerned to see the spiritual needs of believers met and am willing to be personally involved in nurturing and discipling ministries.	☐	☐	☐	☑	☐
20. I like to help people understand things.	☐	☐	☐	☑	☐
21. I am able to make effective plans to accomplish goals.	☐	☐	☐	☑	☐
22. People in the Christian community have been stirred up to love and good works by my counsel and encouragement.	☐	☐	☑	☐	☐
23. I have been instrumental in leading others to believe in Christ as their Savior.	☐	☑	☐	☐	☐
24. In specific cases God has given me assurance that He would do what seemed unlikely.	☐	☑	☐	☐	☐

The Following Is True of Me...	(1) Very Little	(2) Little	(3) Some	(4) Much	(5) Very Much
25. I give cheerfully and liberally in support of the Lord's work.	☐	☐	☑	☐	☐
26. I enjoy leading and directing others toward goals and caring for them for the sake of Christ.	☐	☐	☐	☑	☐
27. I enjoy working with people who suffer physical, mental, or emotional problems.	☐	☐	☐	☑	☐
28. I have proclaimed timely and urgent messages from God's Word.	☐	☑	☐	☐	☐
29. I like to work at little things that help build the body of Christ.	☐	☐	☐	☑	☐
30. I assume responsibility when I see a Christian being led astray.	☐	☐	☑	☐	☐
31. I am able to clarify things for learners (children or adults).	☐	☐	☑	☐	☐
32. I believe that people will grow to spiritual maturity through counsel and instruction from the Word.	☐	☐	☐	☑	☐
33. I have a burden for friends and acquaintances who do not believe in Christ.	☐	☐	☐	☑	☐
34. I have a sense for moments when the "prayer of faith" is needed.	☐	☐	☑	☐	☐
35. I am willing to maintain a lower standard of living in order to benefit God's work with my financial support.	☐	☐	☑	☐	☐
36. The sight of misery makes me want to find a way to express God's love to hurting persons.	☐	☐	☐	☑	☐
37. Given the opportunity, I would like to be an expository preacher of God's Word.	☐	☐	☑	☐	☐

The Following Is True of Me...	(1) Very Little	(2) Little	(3) Some	(4) Much	(5) Very Much
38. It is my nature to like to do work that helps others do theirs.	❏	❏	❏	☑	❏
39. I sense in myself a shepherd's instinct when I know of Christians who need spiritual counsel.	❏	❏	❏	☑	❏
40. I quickly sense when people (children or adults) are unclear in their thinking.	❏	❏	☑	❏	❏
41. I have a sense for delegating important tasks to the right people at the right time.	❏	❏	☑	❏	❏
42. I am glad when people who need comfort, consolation, encouragement, and counsel seek my help.	❏	❏	❏	☑	❏
43. I am able to share the gospel in a way that makes it clear and meaningful to nonbelievers.	❏	❏	☑	❏	❏
44. I am able to go on believing God will act in a situation in spite of evidence to the contrary.	❏	❏	❏	☑	❏
45. I help people and the Lord's work through generous and timely contributions.	❏	❏	☑	❏	❏
46. I have accepted leadership responsibilities and have succeeded in helping a group work toward a goal.	❏	❏	❏	☑	❏
47. Sick, helpless, and shut-in persons are helped when I minister to them.	❏	❏	☑	❏	❏
48. God uses me to build up, encourage, and comfort other Christians by speaking to them of spiritual things.	❏	❏	❏	☑	❏
49. I find practical ways of helping others and gain satisfaction from doing this.	❏	❏	❏	☑	❏

	(1) Very Little	(2) Little	(3) Some	(4) Much	(5) Very Much

The Following Is True of Me...

50. The Lord has used me to watch over, guide, and nurture other believers toward spiritual maturity. — (3) Some

51. I hold the interest of those I teach. — (4) Much

52. I would be willing to spend some time each week in a counseling ministry. — (3) Some

53. I am able to sense when a person doesn't know Jesus Christ, and I hurt for him or her. — (4) Much

54. I inwardly sense what Jesus meant when he said mountains could be moved by faith. — (2) Little

55. I have a conviction that all I have belongs to God, and I want to be a good steward. — (3) Some

56. I sense when people are hurting in some way. — (4) Much

57. I think more Christians should speak out on the moral issues of the day, such as abortion, easy sex, racism, and so on. — (4) Much

58. I wish I had more opportunity to assist others in their ministries. — (3) Some

59. I would love to be in a position to equip saints for the work of ministry. — (4) Much

60. I get excited about discovering new ideas I can share with others. — (4) Much

KEY CHART

1	21	41	6	26	46	Administration/Leadership
4	4	3	3	4	4	22
2	22	42	12	32	52	Exhortation
3	3	4	4	4	3	21
3	23	43	13	33	53	Evangelism
3	2	3	4	4	4	20
4	24	44	14	34	54	Faith
2	2	4	4	3	2	17
5	25	45	15	35	55	Giving
3	3	3	3	3	3	18
7	27	47	16	36	56	Mercy
3	4	3	4	4	4	22
8	28	48	17	37	57	Prophecy
3	2	4	2	3	4	18
9	29	49	18	38	58	Serving
4	4	4	4	4	3	23
10	30	50	19	39	59	Shepherding
3	3	3	4	4	4	21
11	31	51	20	40	60	Teaching
3	3	4	4	3	4	21

HOW TO USE THE KEY CHART

1. Each of the boxes above has a number that corresponds to one of the statements on pages 98-102. In each box record the numerical value (1-5) you assigned to that statement.

2. Working across each row, add up the six numbers you just entered and record the total under the name of the spiritual gift on that row.

3. Circle the three highest scores and write the corresponding gifts in the Results Box on page 104.

RESULTS BOX

Highest score   _SERVING_

Second highest   _MERCY_

Third highest   _ADMINISTRATION / LEADERSHIP_

These may be your spiritual gifts. Turn back to page 81 of chapter 7 for further instructions on how to identify your spiritual gifts.

APPENDIX D
APPRENTICESHIP VEHICLES

The following paragraphs offer ideas of areas where the possession of each spiritual gift could be assessed. These suggestions are meant to stimulate your creative genius rather than provide an exhaustive catalog of possibilities.

PROPHECY

The local rescue mission provides an excellent opportunity to test for this gift. Try preaching there. Or take on a short series in prayer meeting. Other possibilities are to speak to the young people as a short-term youth worker or to lead a Sunday school class. The prayer meeting or Sunday school class offers the most consistent concentrated opportunity, but do not discount the mission—it outweighs all the other areas in my opinion.

EVANGELISM

Most of the vehicles for apprenticeship in this area are already in operation within your church. Your church's ministry to a rescue mission, jail, or nursing home provides excellent opportunities for the evaluation of the gift of evangelism on both the personal and corporate levels. Child Evangelism Fellowship, after-school clubs, Daily Vacation Bible School, and children's church are other areas for experimentation. About the most logical place to start your apprenticeship is the weekly visitation program of your church.[1] Or you could fill your pockets with tracts and head for the nearest street corner.

SHEPHERDING

If there is a shortage of the exercise of any particular gift within the local church, it is this one. A pastor quickly realizes that he cannot do everything that needs to be done, be everything he needs to be, and go every place he needs to go to meet all the needs of the congregation. The wise pastor must look for those within the congregation with the gift of shepherding and start cultivating them to share the load. Inspiring others to exercise this gift is one key to an effective ministry. A church should have a plan for developing cell leaders and small group leaders who will "pastor" small groups of people. Implementing such a plan is the only way a church can grow past the two-hundred-member barrier. Otherwise climbing past this level is virtually impossible.

Whether or not your church has such a plan, you could serve as a shepherding apprentice in tandem with the sponsors for your youth groups. You could care for widows, shut-ins, and the elderly. You could oversee any small group: Sunday school class, home Bible study, neighborhood cell group, or nursing home visitation team. You could disciple new converts, either one-on-one or in groups.

TEACHING

This is an easy gift to test for because of the many vehicles available in any church. You could teach in Sunday school classes, children's church programs, youth programs, nursery programs, after-school club, or prayer meeting. You could also disciple new converts.

EXHORTATION

Ready-made areas where this gift functions are deacon-care, nursing home, and hospital visitation ministries. Apprenticeships could be set up in the areas of counseling and encouraging the bereaved, depressed, sick, and oppressed.

FAITH

An apprenticeship could be set up in conjunction with a planning or building committee. Or a prayer ministry could be structured to test for this gift. You and your mentor would need to arrange for a regular, consistent prayer time; prepare a specific agenda including projects and needs for which to pray; and keep an accurate prayer journal with specific requests and dates in one column and answers with dates in another column. God does not always answer in the allotted four weeks, but the types of prayers you offer and the answers you expect will indicate the presence or absence of the gift of faith.

HELPS/MINISTERING

You could start to develop a testing vehicle by compiling a list of jobs that need to be done in order to free up people who have other gifts; for instance, typing stencils and running off bulletins could free up a church leader to exercise his gift of administration. Your list will probably keep you busy for more than four weeks! The jobs may include preparing crafts for children's church, driving the van for senior citizens, filing, cataloging, telephoning, preparing a mailing, or setting up chairs for Sunday school. For a person already involved in ministry these extra jobs are burdens, but for a server they are welcome opportunities.

GIVING

An apprenticeship in giving should include exposure to needy members of the family of God. Needy Christians may be found, for example, in a deacon-care program or senior citizen ministry, or among widows and shut-ins. An apprenticeship should include a period of time during which you trust God to supply a certain amount above and beyond your regular giving to meet a particular need laid upon your heart. Keep a journal so that at the end of the period, if you truly possess the gift, you can see how God has met the need through the exercise of your gift.

ADMINISTRATION/LEADERSHIP

Any organizational task can provide an opportunity to test for this gift. You could try organizing part of an annual project such as family day, the Sunday school picnic, a missionary conference, an advertising campaign, or a neighborhood canvassing blitz. You could plan youth outings and socials or run a visitation program.

MERCY

As needs arise, they should be worked into an apprenticeship in showing mercy. These needs might be a death in a family, an illness, a calamity—anything that causes people to hurt. You could comfort those in need or participate in regular hospital visitation, nursing home visitation, and visitation of shut-ins. On prayer meeting evenings take note when illnesses or special needs are mentioned and incorporate them into your apprenticeship.

Appendix E

Evaluation Tool

This appendix consists of assessment forms—one for each of the spiritual gifts that are for today. You have permission from the publisher to make enough copies of the appropriate form so that you and your mentor can fill out separate sheets at the end of each opportunity to exercise a gift. At the end of an apprenticeship you and your mentor should evaluate all the sheets that have been filled out.

ASSESSMENT OF APPRENTICE

GIFT OF PROPHECY

Apprentice:_____ Mentor:_____

Assessment prepared by:_____

Activity:_____ Date:_____

1. Assessment of Performance
   Did apprentice exhibit any of the following characteristics?
   A person possessing the gift of prophecy...
   • adheres fearlessly to the truth of God's Word.
   • is outspoken, clear-cut, decisive.
   • motivates others to holiness of life.
   • sees only black and white.

2. Assessment of Product
   Did you observe any of the following results?
   People comprehended what God is saying.
   People were convinced that what the apprentice said
      is what the passage of Scripture is teaching.
   People conformed their lives to the Biblical standard.

3. Comments

   _____

   _____

   _____

   _____

ASSESSMENT OF APPRENTICE

GIFT OF EVANGELISM

Apprentice:_____ Mentor:_____

Assessment prepared by:_____

Activity:_____ Date:_____

1. Assessment of Performance
   Did apprentice exhibit any of the following characteristics?
   A person possessing the gift of evangelism...
   • has a burning desire for the lost to be saved.
   • witnesses frequently.
   • has a unilateral emphasis: the lost.
   • engages in much prayer for the lost.

2. Assessment of Product
   Did you observe any of the following results?
   People were convicted by the Holy Spirit.
   People were converted.

3. Comments

   _____

   _____

   _____

   _____

ASSESSMENT OF APPRENTICE

GIFT OF SHEPHERDING

Apprentice:_____ Mentor:_____

Assessment prepared by:_____

Activity:_____ Date:_____

1. Assessment of Performance
    Did apprentice exhibit any of the following characteristics?
    A person possessing the gift of shepherding…
    • shows genuine care for the flock.
    • has a feeling of possession—uses the pronoun *my*.
    • has made a long-term commitment to the flock.
    • has set a goal for the flock: maturity in Christ.
    • is able to solve problems between people.
    • requires an outlet—shepherd to sheep.

2. Assessment of Product
    Did you observe any of the following results?
    People in the flock were edified.
    They made measurable progress toward maturity.
    They have unswerving confidence in the shepherd.
    They know they are being fed.

3. Comments

    _____

    _____

    _____

    _____

ASSESSMENT OF APPRENTICE

GIFT OF TEACHING

Apprentice:_____ Mentor:_____

Assessment prepared by:_____

Activity:_____ Date:_____

1. Assessment of Performance
   Did apprentice exhibit any of the following characteristics?
   A person possessing the gift of teaching...
   - analyzes and systematizes Biblical truth.
   - engages in research to prove truth.
   - produces more material than can ever be covered in
     one class.
   - spends time in word studies to ensure accuracy of
     information to be presented.
   - organizes lesson material.

2. Assessment of Product
   Did you observe any of the following results?
   Apprentice's teaching was effective—students learned.
   Students said, "I see what he/she means."
   Students made measurable progress toward maturity.
   Students increased their Bible knowledge.

3. Comments

   _____

   _____

   _____

   _____

ASSESSMENT OF APPRENTICE

GIFT OF EXHORTATION

Apprentice:_____ Mentor:_____
Assessment prepared by:_____
Activity:_____ Date:_____

1. Assessment of Performance
    Did apprentice exhibit any of the following characteristics?
        A person possessing the gift of exhortation...
        • is need-motivated.
        • is able to sense needs in the body.
        • relates better to individuals than groups.
        • emphasizes application of truth.
        • has the ability to size up situations, draw conclu-
          sions, then act on the basis of those conclusions.

2. Assessment of Product
    Did you observe any of the following results?
        People were comforted, exhorted, encouraged.
        People were motivated to action.
        Counselee said, "I'll do that."
        People found his/her counsel valid.

3. Comments

    _____

    _____

    _____

    _____

ASSESSMENT OF APPRENTICE

GIFT OF FAITH

Apprentice:_____ Mentor:_____

Assessment prepared by:_____

Activity:_____ Date:_____

1. Assessment of Performance
    Did apprentice exhibit any of the following characteristics?
    A person possessing the gift of faith…
    - has vision when others don't.
    - believes God for the supplying of needs in a super-
      natural way.
    - has unshakable conviction in the face of the
      "impossible."
    - is interested in the future, not the past.
    - is a goal-centered possibility-thinker.

2. Assessment of Product
    Did you observe any of the following results?
    Apprentice received answers to prayer.
    He/she trusted God for the "impossible."
    He/she was unswerving and straight-ahead in his/her
      approach.

3. Comments

    _____

    _____

    _____

    _____

ASSESSMENT OF APPRENTICE

GIFT OF HELPS/MINISTERING

Apprentice:_____ Mentor:_____

Assessment prepared by:_____

Activity:_____ Date:_____

1. Assessment of Performance
    Did apprentice exhibit any of the following characteristics?
    A person possessing the gift of helps...
    - desires to free up others.
    - is willing to fit in anywhere.
    - is available (his greatest ability is availability).
    - avoids the limelight.
    - prefers a short-term ministry; he is a "jobber."

2. Assessment of Product
    Did you observe any of the following results?
    The body of Christ operated more smoothly.
    Leadership accomplished more.
    More people served in the areas of other gifts.

3. Comments

    _____

    _____

    _____

    _____

GIFT OF GIVING

Apprentice:_____ Mentor:_____

Assessment prepared by:_____

Activity:_____ Date:_____

1. Assessment of Performance
    Did apprentice exhibit any of the following characteristics?
    A person possessing the gift of giving…
    • is motivated by the temporal needs of others.
    • gives more than money—gives self, possessions, and hospitality.
    • has the ability to give extraordinary amounts of money to the Lord's work.

2. Assessment of Product
    Did you observe any of the following results?
    Those with needs found them met.
    The fellowship experienced a feeling of oneness, family, care.
    Others were spurred on to give also.

3. Comments

    _____

    _____

    _____

    _____

ASSESSMENT OF APPRENTICE

GIFT OF ADMINISTRATION/LEADERSHIP

Apprentice:_____ Mentor:_____

Assessment prepared by:_____

Activity:_____ Date:_____

1. Assessment of Performance
    Did apprentice exhibit any of the following characteristics?
        A person possessing the gift of government...
        • is motivated to care for others.
        • assumes leadership when no other leader is present.
        • is able to organize and motivate people.
        • finds it easy to make decisions.
        • has the ability to delegate.

2. Assessment of Product
    Did you observe any of the following results?
        Goals were set.
        A plan was laid out to achieve the goals.
        People were motivated to work the plan.
        The project is on its way to completion.

3. Comments

    _____

    _____

    _____

    _____

ASSESSMENT OF APPRENTICE

GIFT OF MERCY

Apprentice:_____ Mentor:_____

Assessment prepared by:_____

Activity:_____ Date:_____

1. Assessment of Performance
   Did apprentice exhibit any of the following characteristics?
     A person possessing the gift of mercy...
     • excels in one-on-one relationships.
     • seeks out those in need of help.
     • has a soft heart.
     • is ready to go at a moment's notice.
     • is motivated by the hurts others feel.

2. Assessment of Product
   Did you observe any of the following results?
     People with needs felt great relief and comfort.
     People with needs felt the warmth of being loved and
       cared for.
     Intimate bonds were created between the apprentice
       and the people he/she helped.

3. Comments

_____

_____

_____

_____

NOTES

CHAPTER 1

1. Gerhard Delling, *"artios...katartizo"* in *Theological Dictionary of the New Testament*, ed. Gerhard Friedrich and Gerhard Kittel, 10 vols. (Grand Rapids: Eerdmans, 1964-1976) 1:475-476.
2. Hermann Wolfgang Beyer, *"diakoneo, diakonia, diakonos"* in *Theological Dictionary of the New Testament* 2:86.

CHAPTER 2

1. *Doma* and *dosis* are both derived from *didomi*. See Friedrich Buchsel, *"didomi"* in *Theological Dictionary of the New Testament* II:166-167. For *charismata* see Hans Conzelmann, *"chairo-eucharistos"* in *Theological Dictionary of the New Testament* IX:402-404, especially the footnotes.
2. Quoted by Ronald E. Baxter in *Gifts of the Spirit* (Grand Rapids: Kregel, 1983) 27.
3. C. Peter Wagner, *Your Spiritual Gifts Can Help Your Church Grow* (Glendale, CA: Gospel Light, 1974) 42.
4. H. E. Dana and Julius R. Mantey, *A Manual Grammar of the Greek New Testament* (New York: Macmillan, 1927) 101.
5. Ibid., 107.
6. William F. Arndt and F. William Gingrich, *A Greek-English Lexicon of the New Testament* (Chicago: University of Chicago Press, 1952) 182.
7. Gottlob Schrenk, *"boulomai, boule, boulema"* in *Theological Dictionary of the New Testament* 1:635.
8. John R. Stott, *Baptism and Fullness* (Downers Grove, IL: InterVarsity Press, 1977) 111.
9. Leonard I. Sweet, *New Life in the Spirit* (Philadelphia: Westminster, 1982) 78.
10. Earl P. McQuay, *Your Spiritual Gift Has Arrived* (Denver: Accent, 1975) 22-23.

CHAPTER 3

1. Lester Sumrall, *Gifts and Ministries of the Holy Spirit* (Tulsa: Harrison House, 1982) 54.
2. Ralph M. Riggs, *The Spirit Himself* (Springfield, MO: Gospel Publishing House, 1949) 113.
3. Quoted by G. Raymond Carlson in *Spiritual Dynamics* (Springfield, MO: Gospel Publishing House, 1976) 100.
4. Wagner, *Your Spiritual Gifts,* 57.
5. Quoted by Baxter in *Gifts of the Spirit,* 27.
6. Spiritual gifts are much more than talents or innate abilities. The difference is seen, for example, in the product. A spiritual gift, when used, involves not only the person who possesses the gift but the receiver of the service as well. When for instance someone with the gift of evangelism preaches, there are multiple results—thousands come forward when Billy Graham preaches. When another Christian with a mere talent for public speaking preaches an evangelistic message, he only snags a few fish. So a talent is different from a spiritual gift. However, God could give a spiritual gift to a person in an area where he has innate abilities.

CHAPTER 4

1. Baxter, *Gifts of the Spirit,* 101.
2. W. A. Criswell, *The Holy Spirit in Today's World* (Grand Rapids: Zondervan, 1966) 166.
3. McQuay, *Your Spiritual Gift,* 25-26.
4. James M. Gray, "Evangelist," *International Standard Bible Encyclopedia,* ed. James Orr, 5 vols. (Grand Rapids: Eerdmans, 1939) 2:1039.
5. Gerhard Friedrich, *"euangelizomai, euangelion"* in *Theological Dictionary of the New Testament* 2:710-711.
6. Ibid. 2:708.
7. Ibid. 2:720.
8. John E. Walvoord, *The Holy Spirit* (Grand Rapids: Zondervan, 1976) 170.
9. Gray, *International Standard Bible Encyclopedia* 2:1040.
10. Walvoord, "Contemporary Issues in the Doctrine of the Holy Spirit," *Bibliotheca Sacra* 130 (October 1973) 170.
11. John B. Packo, *Find and Use Your Spiritual Gifts* (Harrisburg, PA: Christian Publications, 1967) 65.

12. William McRae, *The Dynamics of Spiritual Gifts* (Grand Rapids: Zondervan, 1976) 56.

13. McQuay, *Your Spiritual Gift,* 26.

14. Leslie B. Flynn, *Nineteen Gifts of the Spirit* (Wheaton, IL: Victor, 1980) 57.

15. Gray, *International Standard Bible Encyclopedia* 2:1040.

16. Ibid.

17. McRae, *Dynamics of Spiritual Gifts,* 56.

18. Packo, *Find and Use,* 65.

19. Flynn, *Nineteen Gifts,* 63.

20. Packo, *Find and Use,* 65-66.

21. Joachim Jeremias, *"poimen"* in *Theological Dictionary of the New Testament* 6:486-487.

22. Flynn, *Nineteen Gifts,* 67-69.

23. Charles Caldwell Ryrie, *Biblical Theology of the New Testament* (Chicago: Moody Press, 1959) 195.

24. Walvoord, *Bibliotheca Sacra* 130:170.

25. Packo, *Find and Use,* 67-68.

26. McQuay, *Your Spiritual Gift,* 27.

27. Wagner, *Your Spiritual Gifts,* 262.

28. Packo, *Find and Use,* 68.

29. Ibid.

30. McQuay, *Your Spiritual Gift,* 57.

31. Karl Heinrich Rengstorf, *"didasko"* in *Theological Dictionary of the New Testament* 2:135.

32. Walvoord, *Bibliotheca Sacra* 130:316.

33. Paul M. Zehr, "The Gifts of the Holy Spirit," *Encounter with the Holy Spirit,* ed. George R. Brunk III (Scottdale, PA: Herald, 1972) 53.

34. McQuay, *Your Spiritual Gift,* 27.

35. Walvoord, *Holy Spirit,* 168.

36. Alfred Plummer, "Teacher," *Dictionary of the Apostolic Church,* ed. James Orr, 2 vols. (Grand Rapids: Baker, 1973) 2:550.

37. M. Scott Fletcher, "Teaching," *Dictionary of the Apostolic Church* 2:552.

38. Flynn, *Nineteen Gifts,* 69.

39. Arndt and Gingrich, *Greek-English Lexicon of New Testament,* 190.

40. Rengstorf, *"didasko"* in *Theological Dictionary of the New Testament* 2:165.

41. Wagner, *Your Spiritual Gifts,* 127.

42. McRae, *Dynamics of Spiritual Gifts,* 48.

43. Packo, *Find and Use,* 36-37.

44. McRae, *Dynamics of Spiritual Gifts,* 48ff.

45. Granville Sharpe's Law with the copulative *kai.*

46. Walvoord, *Holy Spirit,* 120.

47. Packo, *Find and Use,* 68.

48. McRae, *Dynamics of Spiritual Gifts,* 59.

49. Ryrie, *Biblical Theology,* 195.

50. Walvoord does not look at the gift of shepherding apart from the office of pastor. (See Walvoord, *Holy Spirit,* 170.) My contention is that if there were no singular gift of shepherding, there would not be two separate gifts to combine.

51. H. E. Jacobs, "Comfort," *International Standard Bible Encyclopedia* 2:678.

52. Arndt and Gingrich, *Greek-English Lexicon of New Testament,* 622-623.

53. Otto Schmitz, *"parakaleo, parakalesis"* in *Theological Dictionary of the New Testament* 5:796.

54. Ibid. 5:797.

55. Ibid. 5:787.

56. Ibid. 5:776.

57. Ibid. 5:777.

58. Ryrie, *Biblical Theology,* 195.

59. Wagner, *Your Spiritual Gifts,* 154.

60. Packo, *Find and Use,* 38-39.

61. McQuay, *Your Spiritual Gift,* 78.

62. Church Development Resources, *Discover Your Gifts - Workbook,* 3rd ed. (Grand Rapids: CRC Home Missions, 1983) 56.

63. Jacobs, *International Standard Bible Encyclopedia* 2:678.

64. Schmitz, *Theological Dictionary of the New Testament* 5:782.

65. Wagner, *Your Spiritual Gifts,* 154.

66. Packo, *Find and Use,* 38-39.

CHAPTER 5

1. J. I. Packer, *Keep in Step with the Spirit* (Old Tappan, NJ: Revell, 1984) 84.

2. Sumrall, *Gifts and Ministries,* 83.

3. Zehr, *Encounter with Holy Spirit,* 53-54.

4. Anthony D. Palma, *The Spirit—God in Action* (Springfield, MO: Gospel Publishing House, 1974) 83.

5. Carlson, *Spiritual Dynamics,* 103.

6. Ryrie, *Biblical Theology,* 195.

7. McQuay, *Your Spiritual Gift,* 30.

8. McRae, *Dynamics of Spiritual Gifts,* 66.

9. Packo, *Find and Use,* 51.

10. Ibid.

11. McRae, *Dynamics of Spiritual Gifts,* 66.

12. Sumrall, *Gifts and Ministries,* 250.

13. Arndt and Gingrich, *Greek-English Lexicon of New Testament,* 74.

14. Michael Griffiths, *Grace-Gifts* (Grand Rapids: Eerdmans, 1978) 53.

15. Packo, *Find and Use,* 34-35.

16. Wagner, *Your Spiritual Gifts,* 225.

17. Flynn, *Nineteen Gifts,* 101.

18. Beyer, *"diakoneo, diakonia, diakonos"* in *Theological Dictionary of the New Testament* 2:83-84.

19. Ibid.

20. Arndt and Gingrich, *Greek-English Lexicon of New Testament,* 183.

21. Ryrie, *Biblical Theology,* 195.

22. Beyer, *"diakoneo, diakonia, diakonos"* in *Theological Dictionary of the New Testament* 2:87.

23. Walvoord, *Holy Spirit,* 196.

24. Wagner, *Your Spiritual Gifts,* 226.

25. Frank M. Boyd, *The Spirit Works Today* (Springfield, MO: Gospel Publishing House, 1970) 120.

26. *Discover Your Gifts,* 74.

27. McRae, *Dynamics of Spiritual Gifts,* 478.

28. Wagner, *Your Spiritual Gifts,* 260.

29. Ryrie, *Biblical Theology,* 195.

30. McQuay, *Your Spiritual Gift,* 31-32.

31. Packo, *Find and Use,* 41.

32. McRae, *Dynamics of Spiritual Gifts,* 80.

33. *Discover Your Gifts,* 62.

34. Arndt and Gingrich, *Greek-English Lexicon of New Testament,* 85.

35. Friedrich Bauernfeind, *"haplous, haplotes"* in *Theological Dictionary of the New Testament* 1:386-387.

36. Arndt and Gingrich, *Greek-English Lexicon of New Testament,* 85.

37. McQuay, *Your Spiritual Gift,* 32.

38. Bo Reicke, *"proistemi"* in *Theological Dictionary of the New Testament* 6:700-701.
39. Ibid.
40. Beyer, *"kubernesis"* in *Theological Dictionary of the New Testament* 3:1035.
41. Alfred Plummer, "Governments," *Dictionary of the Apostolic Church* 2:507.
42. Buchsel, *"hegeomai"* in *Theological Dictionary of the New Testament* 2:907-908.
43. James Hope Moulton and George Milligan, *The Vocabulary of the Greek New Testament* (Grand Rapids: Eerdmans, 1972) 277.
44. Ryrie, *Biblical Theology,* 195.
45. Stott, *Baptism and Fullness,* 95.
46. McQuay, *Your Spiritual Gift,* 32.
47. Packo, *Find and Use,* 42.
48. Walvoord, *Bibliotheca Sacra* 130:316-317.
49. Wagner, *Your Spiritual Gifts,* 156.
50. McRae, *Dynamics of Spiritual Gifts,* 52.
51. Packo, *Find and Use,* 42-43.
52. Gunther Harder, *"spoudazo, spoude"* in *Theological Dictionary of the New Testament* 7:559.
53. Ibid. 7:566.
54. Rudolph Bultmann, *"eleos"* in *Theological Dictionary of the New Testament* 2:483.
55. R. S. Frands, "Mercy," *Dictionary of the Apostolic Church* 2:29.
56. McQuay, *Your Spiritual Gift,* 32.
57. McRae, *Dynamics of Spiritual Gifts,* 53.
58. Ryrie, *Biblical Theology,* 195.
59. Packo, *Find and Use,* 44.
60. Wagner, *Your Spiritual Gifts,* 260.
61. Arndt and Gingrich, *Greek-English Lexicon of New Testament,* 376.
62. Bultmann, *"lupe"* in *Theological Dictionary of the New Testament* 4:318.
63. Arndt and Gingrich, *Greek-English Lexicon of New Testament,* 483.
64. Ibid., 52.
65. Wagner, *Your Spiritual Gifts,* 223.
66. McQuay, *Your Spiritual Gift,* 33.
67. McRae, *Dynamics of Spiritual Gifts,* 53.
68. Packo, *Find and Use,* 45.

CHAPTER 6

1. McRae, *Dynamics of Spiritual Gifts,* 49ff.
2. Walvoord, *Bibliotheca Sacra* 130:317.
3. Walvoord, *Holy Spirit,* 170.
4. Fletcher, "Exhortation," *Dictionary of the Apostolic Church* 3:383.
5. Wagner, *Your Spiritual Gifts,* 158-159.

CHAPTER 7

1. If a church is healthy and growing only when all the parts of the body are functioning, one of the primary tasks of leadership must be to "make sure every member of the church discovers, develops, and uses his/her spiritual gifts....God does not bring people into the Body of Christ as spectators" (Wagner, *Your Spiritual Gifts,* 132). God does not stock churches with spare parts. Perhaps the first group church leaders need to tap is the senior citizens. Titus 2 shows the tremendous contribution older people can make to the body. There is no retirement from God's service; we are meant to go with our boots on!
2. Wagner, *Your Spiritual Gifts,* 132.
3. McQuay, *Your Spiritual Gift,* 42.
4. Dr. Tim LaHaye's Gift Analysis is a very precise, accurate tool, but may be out of a couple's price range (San Diego: Christian Heritage College).
5. The test in appendix C is an adaptation of "Gifts Analysis Questionnaire" on pages 32-37 of *Discover Your Gifts.*

APPENDIX A

1. Arndt and Gingrich, *Greek-English Lexicon of New Testament,* 89.
2. Rengstorf said, "The activity of the teacher is needed only when that of the apostles and prophets has laid the foundation for the construction of a Christian outlook and manner of life" (Rengstorf, *"didaskalos"* in *Theological Dictionary of the New Testament* 2:158). From the order in which these gifts are mentioned in Ephesians 4:11 he concluded that the work of the apostle is carried out now in the office of the evangelist and the work of the prophet (primary sense) is continued in the office of the pastor/teacher.
3. The gift of word of knowledge is defined in various ways. Criswell said, "A 'word of knowledge' is the ability to grasp the truth about

a present situation" (Criswell, *Holy Spirit*, 172). Packo referred to the gift as follows: "ability to analyze and systematize Biblical truth... ability to be a theologian...ability to study and interpret difficult passages of Scripture...always reflects an in-depth treatment of the subject...finds its expression in research and scholarly work" (Packo, *Find and Use*, 49-50). These definitions seem to refer to individual effort as opposed to a sovereign gift of the Holy Spirit of God. To study and interpret difficult passages in Scripture takes knowledge of the original texts, good study books, and hard work instead of a particular gift. As defined, this gift seems superfluous, since its function seems better categorized under the gift of teaching. Donald Gee said that both word of knowledge and word of wisdom are teaching gifts (*Concerning Spiritual Gifts*, Springfield, MO: Gospel Publishing House, n.d., 112). Packo defined word of wisdom as "the Spirit-given ability to wisely apply knowledge of the Word of God to a given situation. It is seen in the ability to study the Bible and find principles to apply to life...in giving answers to heated debate that relieves tension...the ability to see through a situation when others cannot" (Packo, *Find and Use*, 48-49).

Horton did not link word of knowledge with teaching at all. He saw four present-day uses for this gift: "1. It is a mighty aid in effectual prayer. 2. It is an aid in discovering lost persons or property. 3. It reveals causes of sicknesses or demon-possession. 4. It reveals facts in private lives for spiritual correction" (Harold Horton, *The Gifts of the Spirit*, Bedfordshire, England: Redemption Tidings Bookroom, 1946, pp. 53ff.). This definition might lead you to believe the possessor of the gift is a combination of fortuneteller and witch doctor! Many other definitions of this gift give a quite different impression.

Sumrall, a strong proponent of the existence of all the gifts today, wrote: "Word of knowledge is the revealing of a fact in existence that only could be supernaturally revealed. Word of wisdom is the revealing of a fact about the future which can only be supernaturally revealed....It is supernatural revelation of the Divine purpose of God ... divine communication, a message to the Church from God given by the Holy Spirit through the believer....Any person who speaks out in church, foretelling the future, has left the simple gift of prophecy—the least of all the gifts—and has moved into the greatest and foremost revelatory gift—the word of wisdom whereby he sees the future" (Sumrall,

Gifts and Ministries, 57,59-60). This has to be one of the most blatant aberrations of Scriptural truth ever penned! Sumrall rightly connected word of wisdom with the transmission of revelation.

4. Riggs, *The Spirit Himself,* 122ff.
5. Carlson, *Spiritual Dynamics,* 102.
6. Paul Elbert, "Calvin and the Spiritual Gifts," *Journal of the Evangelical Theological Society* 22 (September 1979) 242.
7. J. W. Jepson, *What You Should Know about the Holy Spirit* (Van Nuys, CA: Bible Voice Books, 1975) 116.
8. Baxter, *Gifts of the Spirit,* 108.
9. McRae, *Dynamics of Spiritual Gifts,* 65ff.
10. Ibid., 57.
11. Baxter, *Gifts of the Spirit,* 103.
12. Quoted by McRae in *Dynamics of Spiritual Gifts,* 65ff.
13. Barclay M. Newman Jr., "Greek-English Dictionary of the New Testament," *The Greek New Testament,* ed. Kurt Aland et al. (Westphalia, England: United Bible Societies, 1975) 42.
14. Arndt and Gingrich, *Greek-English Lexicon of New Testament,* 184.
15. The gift of discernment is described in a variety of ways: "It is the ability to distinguish the spirit of error from the spirit of truth before this difference is manifested to all by its results" (McQuay, *Your Spiritual Gift,* 33). John Calvin defined the gift as the "ability to make piercing judgments between true and false ministers" (Elbert, *Journal of the Evangelical Theological Society* 22:244). "It is the power to distinguish [between] the operation of the Spirit of God, evil spirits, and unassisted human spirits" (Carlson, *Spiritual Dynamics,* 103). "It is the ability to discern whether information which claims to be of God is Satanic, human, or Divine....It exposes error, reveals false prophecy, exorcises demons" (Packo, *Find and Use,* 58-59). "It helps in delivering the afflicted, opposed, and tormented; it is used to discern a servant of the Devil...aids in checking plans of an adversary...used to unmask demon miracle-workers" (Horton, *Gifts of the Spirit,* 53). It is limited to discerning "demon activity and possession" (Riggs, *The Spirit Himself,* 136). "It is only used as the occasion demands, [such as] when confrontation is made with someone who may be demon-possessed or demonically deceived" (McQuay, *Your Spiritual Gift,* 33). "It is the comprehending of the human spirit, whether good or bad, not discerning of demons....It is not

primarily a divining rod to root out demons, but the ability to discern the human spirit" (Sumrall, *Gifts and Ministries,* 57,75).

16. J. C. Lambert, "Spiritual Gifts," *International Standard Bible Encyclopedia* 2:2843.

17. Ryrie, *Biblical Theology,* 195.

18. Walvoord, *The Holy Spirit,* 188.

19. Baxter, *Gifts of the Spirit,* 112.

20. J. Oswald Sanders, *The Holy Spirit and His Gifts* (Grand Rapids: Zondervan, 1940) 120.

21. McRae, *Dynamics of Spiritual Gifts,* 73ff.

22. Arndt and Gingrich, *Greek-English Lexicon of New Testament,* 201.

APPENDIX B

1. Gustav Stahlin, *"xenos"* in *Theological Dictionary of the New Testament* 5:30.

2. Packo, *Find and Use,* 79-80.

3. *Discover Your Gifts,* 64.

4. Wagner, *Your Spiritual Gifts,* 263.

5. Albrecht Oepke, *"onar"* in *Theological Dictionary of the New Testament* 5:230.

6. Arndt and Gingrich, *Greek-English Lexicon of New Testament,* 163.

7. Wagner, *Your Spiritual Gifts,* 74.

8. Ibid., 96.

9. Ibid., 67.

10. Packo, *Find and Use,* 45.

APPENDIX D

1. See James Kennedy, *Evangelism Explosion* (Wheaton, IL: Tyndale, 1970).

BIBLIOGRAPHY

Aland, Kurt, et al., ed. *The Greek New Testament.* Westphalia, England: United Bible Societies, 1975.

Arndt, William F., and F. William Gingrich. *A Greek-English Lexicon of the New Testament.* Chicago: University of Chicago Press, 1952.

Baxter, Ronald E. *The Charismatic Gift of Tongues.* Grand Rapids: Baker, 1974.

————. *Gifts of the Spirit.* Grand Rapids: Kregel, 1983.

Boyd, Frank M. *The Spirit Works Today.* Springfield, MO: Gospel Publishing House, 1970.

Carlson, G. Raymond. *Spiritual Dynamics.* Springfield, MO: Gospel Publishing House, 1976.

Church Development Resources. *Discover Your Gifts.* 3rd rev. ed. Grand Rapids: CRC Home Missions, 1983.

Criswell, W. A. *The Holy Spirit in Today's World.* Grand Rapids: Zondervan, 1966.

Dana, H. E., and Julius R. Mantey. *A Manual Grammar of the Greek New Testament.* New York: Macmillan, 1927.

Dunn, James D. G. *Baptism in the Holy Spirit.* London: SCM, 1970.

Elbert, Paul. "Calvin and the Spiritual Gifts." *Journal of the Evangelical Theological Society* 22 (September 1979) 235-256.

Flynn, Leslie B. *Nineteen Gifts of the Spirit.* Wheaton: Victor, 1980.

Friedrich, Gerhard, and Gerhard Kittel, eds. *Theological Dictionary of the New Testament.* 10 vols. Grand Rapids: Eerdmans, 1964-1976.

Gee, Donald. *Concerning Spiritual Gifts.* Springfield, MO: Gospel Publishing House, n.d.

Griffiths, Michael. *Grace-Gifts.* Grand Rapids: Eerdmans, 1978.

Harper, Michael. *Life in the Spirit.* Plainfield, NJ: Logos, n.d.

Horton, Harold. *The Gifts of the Spirit.* Bedfordshire, England: Redemption Tidings Bookroom, 1946.

Jepson, J. W. *What You Should Know about the Holy Spirit.* Van Nuys, CA: Bible Voice Books, 1975.

MacGavran, J. W. *The Gifts of the Spirit.* Nashville: Broadman, 1974.

McQuay, Earl P. *Your Spiritual Gift Has Arrived.* Denver: Accent, 1975.

McRae, William. *The Dynamics of Spiritual Gifts.* Grand Rapids: Zondervan, 1976.

Metzger, Bruce M. *A Textual Commentary on the Greek New Testament.* New York: United Bible Societies, 1971.

Mickelsen, A. Berkley. *Interpreting the Bible.* Grand Rapids: Eerdmans, 1963.

Moulton, James Hope, and George Milligan. *The Vocabulary of the Greek New Testament.* Grand Rapids: Eerdmans, 1972.

Newell, William B. *Romans Verse by Verse.* Chicago: Moody Press, 1947.

Orr, James, ed. *Dictionary of the Apostolic Church.* 2 vols. Grand Rapids: Baker, 1973.

———, ed. *International Standard Bible Encyclopedia.* 5 vols. Grand Rapids: Eerdmans, 1939.

Packer, J. I. *Keep in Step with the Spirit.* Old Tappan, NJ: Revell, 1984.

Packo, John B. *Find and Use Your Spiritual Gifts.* Harrisburg, PA: Christian Publications, 1967.

Palma, Anthony D. *The Spirit—God in Action.* Springfield, MO: Gospel Publishing House, 1974.

Riggs, Ralph M. *The Spirit Himself.* Springfield, MO: Gospel Publishing House, 1949.

Ryrie, Charles Caldwell. *Biblical Theology of the New Testament.* Chicago: Moody Press, 1959.

———. *The Holy Spirit.* Chicago: Moody Press, 1976.

Sanders, J. Oswald. *The Holy Spirit and His Gifts.* Grand Rapids: Zondervan, 1940.

Stott, John R. *Baptism and Fullness.* Downers Grove, IL: InterVarsity Press, 1977.

Sumrall, Lester. *Gifts and Ministries of the Holy Spirit.* Tulsa: Harrison House, 1982.

Sweet, Leonard I. *New Life in the Spirit.* Philadelphia: Westminster, 1982.

Wagner, C. Peter. *Your Spiritual Gifts Can Help Your Church Grow.* Glendale, CA: Gospel Light, 1974.

Walvoord, John E. "Contemporary Issues in the Doctrine of the Holy Spirit." *Bibliotheca Sacra* 130 (October 1973) 315-328.

———. *The Holy Spirit.* Grand Rapids: Zondervan, 1976.

Wuest, Kenneth. *Word Studies in the Greek New Testament.* Vol. 1. Grand Rapids: Eerdmans, n.d.

Zehr, Paul M. "The Gifts of the Holy Spirit." *Encounter with the Holy Spirit.* ed. George R. Brunk III. Scottdale, PA: Herald, 1972.

ABOUT THE AUTHOR

❦

D r. Bruce Black holds degrees from Northeastern Bible College (B.A.), Faith Seminary (M.Div.), and Westminster Seminary (D.Min.). He has pastored churches in New Jersey and eastern Pennsylvania for more than twenty years and teaches continuing education courses for Philadelphia College of the Bible. *The Spiritual Gifts Handbook,* his first book, is the product of this pastoral and teaching experience.